"On the one hand, Bell's is an attractive, powerful intervention in the often ugly world of American evangelicalism, an ugliness that via American politics can indirectly damage us all. But it's also a good news story." **Guardian**

"He could be one of the most important 21st-century Christian leaders." **Time**

"Rob Bell is one of the hottest names in contemporary evangelical life." **Boston Globe**

"Time and again, Bell challenges the reader to be open to surprise, mystery, and all of the unanswerables contained within the 'wide stream' called Christianity." **Christian Century**

"Rob Bell is a central figure for his generation and for the way that evangelicals are likely to do church in the next 20 years." **New York Times**

"Bell is one of the most influential Christian leaders in the country." **New Yorker**

WHAT WE TALK ABOUT
WHEN WE TALK
ABOUT GOD

Also by Rob Bell

Love Wins

Velvet Elvis

Sex God

Jesus Wants to Save Christians (with Don Golden)

Drops Like Stars

The Love Wins Companion

ROB BELL

WHAT WE TALK ABOUT WHEN WE TALK ABOUT GOD

FINDING A NEW FAITH FOR THE TWENTY-FIRST CENTURY

Collins

Collins
an imprint of
HarperCollins*Publishers*
77–85 Fulham Palace Road
London W6 8JB

www.collins.co.uk

10 9 8 7 6 5 4 3 2 1

First published in the USA in 2013 by HarperOne
This edition 2013

A catalogue record for this book is
available from the British Library.

ISBN: 978-0-00-742733-8

Printed and bound in Great Britain by Clays Ltd, St Ives plc.

MIX
Paper from
responsible sources
FSC **FSC® C007454**
www.fsc.org

FSC™ is a non-profit international organisation established to promote the
responsible management of the world's forests. Products carrying the FSC
label are independently certified to assure consumers that they come from
forests that are managed to meet the social, economic and ecological needs
of present and future generations, and other controlled sources.

Find out more about HarperCollins and the environment at
www.harpercollins.co.uk/green

Like all great things in the world, women and religion and the sky . . . you wonder about it, and you don't stop wondering about it.

—Tom Waits

CONTENTS

CHAPTER 1

HUH

CHAPTER 1

HUM

I realize that when I use the word *God* in the title of this book there's a good chance I'm stepping on all kinds of land mines. Is there a more volatile word loaded down with more history, assumptions, and expectations than that tired, old, relevant, electrically charged, provocative, fresh, antiquated yet ubiquitous as ever, familiar/ unfamiliar word *God*?

And that's why I use it.

From people risking their lives to serve the poor because they believe God called them to do it, to pastors claiming that the latest tornado or hurricane or earthquake is God's judgment, to professors proclaiming that God has only ever been a figment of our imagination, to people in a recovery meeting sitting in a circle drinking bad coffee and talking about surrendering to a higher power, to musicians in their acceptance speech at an awards show thanking God for their hit song about a late-night booty call, when it comes to God, we are all over the place.

Like a mirror, God appears to be more and more a reflection of whoever it is that happens to be talking about God at the moment.

And then there are the latest surveys and polls, the ones telling us how many of us believe and don't believe in God and how many fewer of us are going to church, inevitably prompting experts to speculate about demographics and technology and worship style and this generation versus that generation, all of it avoiding the glaring truth that sits right there elephant-like in the middle of the room.

The truth is, we have a problem with God.

It's not just a problem of definition—what is it we're talking about when we talk about God?—and it's not just the increasing likelihood that two people discussing God are in fact talking about two extraordinarily different realities while using the exact same word.

This problem with God goes much, much deeper.

As a pastor over the past twenty years, what I've seen again and again is people who want to live lives of meaning and peace and significance and joy—people who have a compelling sense that their spirituality is in some vital and yet mysterious way central to who they are—but who can't find meaning in the dominant conceptions, perceptions, and understandings of God they've encountered. In fact, those conceptions aren't just failing them but are actually causing harm.

We're engaged more than ever by the possibilities of soul and spirit, and by the nagging suspicion that all of this may not be a grand accident after all; but God, an increasing number of people are asking—what does God have to do with *that*?

I've written *this* book about *that* word, then, because there's something in the air, we're in the midst of a massive rethink, a movement is gaining momentum, a moment in history is in the making: there is a growing sense among a growing number of people that when it comes to God, we're at the end of one era and the start of another, an entire mode of understanding and talking about God dying as something new is being birthed.

There's an ancient story about a man named Jacob who had a magnificent dream, and when he wakes up he says, "Surely God was in this place, and I, I wasn't aware of it."

Until now.

The power of the story is its timeless reminder that God hasn't changed; it's Jacob who wakes up to a whole new awareness of who—and where—God is.

Which brings me back to this moment, to the realization among an increasing number of people that we are waking up in new ways to the God who's been here the whole time.

I'm aware, to say the least, that talking about this and writing a book about it, naming it and trying to explain it and taking a shot at describing where it's all headed, runs all sorts of risks.

I get that.

We're surrounded by friends and neighbors and family and intellectual and religious systems with deeply held, vested interests in the conventional categories and conceptions of belief and denial continuing to remain as entrenched as those traditional conceptions are. There are, as they say, snipers on every roof. And being controversial isn't remotely interesting.

But love and meaning and joy and hope?
That's compelling.
That's what I'm after.
That's worth the risk.

The great German scholar Helmut Thielicke once said that a person who speaks to this hour's need will always be skirting the edge of heresy, but only the person who risks those heresies can gain the truth.

And the truth is, we have a problem—we have a *need*—and there's always the chance that this may in fact be the hour.

First, then, a bit more about this God problem . . .

When I was twenty, I drove an Oldsmobile.

Remember those?

It was a four-door Delta 88 and it was silver and it had a bench seat across the front with an armrest that folded down and it fit seven or eight people easily and in a feat of engineering genius the rear license plate was on a hinge that you pulled down in order to fill up the gas tank and the trunk was so huge you could put five snowboards in at the same time or a drum set, several guitar amps, and a body if you needed to. (I'm just messing with you there, about the body.) My friends called it "the Sled."

It was a magnificent automobile, the Sled, and it served me well for those years.

But they don't make Oldsmobiles anymore.

They used to be popular, and your grandparents or roommate may still drive one, but the factories have shut down. Eventually the only ones left will be collector's items, relics of an era that has passed.

Oldsmobile couldn't keep up with the times, and so it gradually became part of the past, not the future.

For them, not us.
For then, not now.

I tell you about the Sled I used to drive because for many in our world today, God is like Oldsmobiles.
To explain what I mean when I talk about God-like Oldsmobiles, a few stories: my friend Cathi recently told me about an event she attended where an influential Christian leader talked openly about how he didn't think women should be allowed to teach and lead in the church. Cathi, who has *two* master's degrees, sat there stunned.

I got an e-mail from my friend Gary last year, saying that he'd decided to visit a church with his family on Easter Sunday. They'd heard a sermon about how resurrection means everybody who is gay is going to hell.

And then my friend Michael recently told me about hearing the leader of a large Christian denomination say that if you deny that God made the world in a literal six days, you are denying the rest of the Bible as well, because it doesn't matter what science says.

And then there are the two pastors I know who each told me, within days of the other, how their wives don't want anything to do with God. Both wives were raised and educated in very religious environments that placed a great deal of importance on the belief that God is good and the point of life is to have a personal relationship with this good God. But both wives have suffered great pain in their young lives, and the clean and neat categories of faith they were handed in their youth haven't been capable of helping them navigate the complexity of their experiences. And so, like jilted lovers, they have turned away. God, for them, is an awkward, alien, strange notion. Like someone they used to know.

And then there's the party I attended in New York where I met a well-known journalist who, when he was told that I'm a pastor, wanted to know if *all of you pastors* use big charts with timelines and graphics to show people when the world is going to end and how Christians are going to escape while those who are left behind endure untold suffering.

I tell you about Cathi sitting there stunned and Gary hearing that sermon and me at that party because whether it's science or art or education or medicine or personal rights or basic intellectual integrity or simply dealing with suffering in all of its complexity, for many in our world—and this includes Christians and a growing number of pastors—believing or trusting in *that* God, the one they've heard other Christians talk about, feels like a step *backward,* to an earlier, less informed and enlightened time, one that we've thankfully left behind.

There's a question that lurks in these stories, a question that an ever-increasing number of people across a broad range of backgrounds and perspectives are asking about God:

Can God keep up with the modern world?

Things have changed. We have more information and technology than ever. We're interacting with a far more diverse range of people than we used to. And the tribal God,
the one that is the only one many have been exposed to—the one who's always right (which means everybody else is wrong)—is increasingly perceived to be
small,
narrow,
irrelevant,
mean,
and sometimes just not that intelligent.

Is God going to be left behind?
Like Oldsmobiles?

––––––––

For others, it isn't that God is behind or unable to deal with the complexity of life; for them God never existed in the first place. In recent years we've heard a number of very intelligent and articulate scientists, professors, and writers argue passionately and confidently that there is no God. This particular faith insists that human beings are nothing more than highly complex interactions of atoms and molecules and neurons, hardwired over time to respond to stimuli in particular ways, feverishly constructing meaning to protect us from the unwelcome truth that there is no ultimate meaning because in the end we are simply the sum of our parts—no more, no less.

That all there is
is, in the end,
all there is.

This denial isn't anything new, but it's gained a head of steam in recent years, this resurgence seemingly in reaction to the God-like Oldsmobile, the one more and more people are becoming convinced is not only *behind,* but downright *destructive.*

I was recently invited to participate in a debate at which the topic was "Is religion good or bad?" Here's the kicker: the organizers wanted me to know I was free to choose which side I'd take!

How revealing is that?

All of which brings me to Jane Fonda. (You didn't see *that* coming, did you?) Several years ago in an interview she gave to *Rolling Stone* magazine the interviewer said this:

> Your most recent—and perhaps most dramatic—
> transformation is your becoming a Christian. Even with your
> flair for controversy, that's pretty explosive.

It's a telling statement, isn't it? You can sense so much there, as if there's a question behind the question that isn't really a question—that hidden question being what the interviewer *really* wants to ask her: "Why would anybody become a Christian?"

That's a question lots of people have—educated, reasonable, modern people who find becoming a Christian an "explosive," not to mention an inconceivable, thing to do.

In her response, Jane Fonda spoke of being drawn to faith because "I could feel reverence humming in me."

Reverence humming in me. I love that phrase. It speaks to the experiences we've all had—moments and tastes and glimpses when we've found ourselves deeply aware of the *something more* of life, the *something else,* the sense that all of this might just mean something, that it may not be an accident, that it has profound resonance and that it matters in ways that are very real and very hard to explain.

For a massive number of people, to deny this reverence humming in us, to insist that we're simply random collections of atoms and that all there is is all there is, leaves them cold, bored, and uninspired.

It doesn't ring true to our very real experiences of life.

But when people turn to many of the conventional, traditional religious explanations for this reverence, they're often led to the God who is like Oldsmobiles, the one who's *back there, behind,* unable to keep up.

All of this raising the questions:
Are there other ways to talk about the reverence humming in us?
Are there other ways to talk about the sense we have that there's way more going on here?
Are there other ways to talk about God?

My answer is yes. I believe there are. But before we get to those others ways, I need to first tell you why this book comes bursting out of my heart like it does.

———

One Sunday morning a number of years ago I found myself face-to-face with the possibility that there is no God and we really are on our own and this may be all there is.

Now I realize lots of people have questions and convictions and doubts along those lines—that's nothing new. But in my case, it was an *Easter* Sunday morning, and I was a *pastor*. I was driving to the church services where I'd be giving a sermon about how there is a God and that God came here to Earth to do something miraculous and rise from the dead so that all of us could live forever.

And it was expected that I would do this passionately and confidently and persuasively with great hope and joy and lots of exclamation points. !!!!!!!

That's how the Easter sermon goes, right? Imagine if I'd stood up there and said, "Well, I've been thinking about this for a while, and I gotta be honest with you: I think we're kinda screwed."

Doesn't work, does it?

I should pause here and say that when you're a pastor, your heart and soul and paycheck and doubts and faith and hopes and struggles and intellect and responsibility are all wrapped up together in a life/job that is very *public*. And Sunday comes once a week, when you're expected to have something inspiring to say, regardless of how you happen to feel or think about God at the moment. This can create a suffocating tension at times, because you want to serve people well and give them your very best, and yet you're also human. And in my case, full of really, really serious doubts about the entire ball of God wax.

That Easter Sunday was fairly traumatic, to say the least, because I realized that without some serious reflection and study and wise counsel I couldn't keep going without losing something vital to my sanity. The only way forward was to plunge headfirst into my doubts and swim all the way to the bottom and find out just how deep that pool went. And if I had to, in the end, walk away in good conscience, then so be it. At least I'd have my integrity.

This book, then, is deeply, deeply personal for me. Much of what I've written here comes directly out of my own doubt, skepticism, and dark nights of the soul when I found myself questioning—to be honest—*everything*. There is a cold shudder that runs down the spine when you find yourself face-to-face with the unvarnished possibility that we may in the end be alone. To trust that there is a divine being who cares and loves and guides can feel like taking a leap—across the ocean. So when I talk about God and faith and belief and all that, it's not from a triumphant, impatient posture of "Come on, people—get with the program!" I come to this topic limping, with some bruises, acutely aware of how maddening, confusing, frustrating, infuriating, and even traumatic it can be to talk about God.

What I experienced, over a long period of time, was a gradual awakening to new perspectives on God—specifically, the God Jesus talked about. I came to see that there were depths and dimensions to the ancient Hebrew tradition, and to the Christian tradition which

grew out of that, that spoke directly to my questions and
struggles in coming to terms with
how to conceive of who God is
and what God is
and why that even matters
and what that has to do with life in this world,
here and now.

Through that process, which is of course still going on,
the doubts didn't suddenly go away and the beliefs didn't
suddenly form nice, neat categories. Something much
more profound happened. Something extraordinarily
freeing and inspiring and invigorating and really, really
helpful, something thrilling which compels me to sit here
day after day, month after month, and write this book.

Which leads me to two brief truths about this book
before we go further.

First, I'm a Christian, and so Jesus is how I understand
God. I realize that for some people, hearing talk about
Jesus shrinks and narrows the discussion about God,
but my experience has been the exact opposite. My
experiences of Jesus have opened my mind and my heart
to a bigger, wider, more expansive and mysterious and
loving God who I believe is actually up to something in
the world.

Second, what I've experienced time and time again is
that people want to talk about God. Whether it's what

they were taught growing up or not taught, or what inspires them or what repulses them, or what gives them hope or what fills them with despair, I've found people to be extremely keen to talk about their beliefs and lack of beliefs in God. What I've observed is that while we want more of a connection with the reverence humming within us, we often don't know where to begin or what steps to take or what that process even looks like.

So if, in some small way, this book could provide some guidance along these lines, I'd be ecstatic. In saying that, I should be clear here about one point: this is not a book in which I'll try to prove that God exists. If you even *could* prove the existence of the divine, I suspect that at that moment you would in fact be talking about something, or somebody, else.

This is a book about seeing, about becoming more and more alive and aware, orienting ourselves around the God who I believe is the ground of our being, the electricity that lights up the whole house, the transcendent presence in our tastes, sights, and sensations of the depth and dimension and fullness of life, from joy to agony to everything else.

_____

Now, about where we're headed in the following pages.

This book centers around three words. They aren't long or technical or complicated or scholarly; they're short, simple, everyday words, and they're the foundation on which everything we're going to cover rests.

These three words are central to how I understand God, and if I could CAPS LOCK THEM THE WHOLE WAY THROUGHOUT THE BOOK, I would; or write them in the sky or etch them in blood (on second thought, maybe not) or graffiti them on the side of your house (let's not do this either, though I'd love to see what Banksy would do with them), because they're the giant, big, loud, this-one-goes-to-eleven idea that animates everything we're going to explore in the following pages.

They've unleashed in me new ways of thinking about and understanding and most importantly *experiencing* God. They've made my life better, and my hope is that they will do the same for you.

But before we get to those three words, we first have two others words we're going to cover. (Nice buildup, huh?)

It's these two words that will set us up for the three words that form the backbone of the book.

First, we'll talk about being **open,** because when we talk about God we drag a massive amount of expectations and assumptions into the discussion with us about how the world works and what kind of universe we're living in. Often God's existence is challenged in the conversation about what matters most in the modern world because haven't we moved past all of that ancient, primitive, superstitious thinking? We have science after all, and reason and logic and evidence. What does God have to do with the new challenges we're facing and knowledge we're acquiring? Quite a lot, actually, because the universe, it turns out, is way, way weirder than any of us first thought. And that weirdness will demand that we be **open.**

So first, **Open.**

Then we'll talk about talking, because when we talk about God, we're using language, and language **both** helps us and fails us in our attempts to understand and describe the paradoxical nature of the God who is beyond words.

First **Open,**
then **Both.**

And then, after those two words,
we get to the three words,
the words that will shape how we talk about God in this book.
The words are (I feel like there should be a drumroll or something . . .)

With,
For,
Ahead.

With, because I understand God to be the energy, the glue, the force, the life, the power, and the source of all we know to be the depth, fullness, and vitality of life from the highest of highs to the lowest of lows and everything in between. I believe God is *with* us because I believe that all of us are already experiencing the presence of God in countless ways every single day. In talking about the God who is with us, I want you to see how this *with*ness directly confronts popular notions of God that put God somewhere else, doing something else, coming here now and again to do God-type things. I want you to see both the irrelevance and the danger of that particular perspective of God as you more and more see God all around you all the time.

Then **for,** because I believe God is *for* every single one of us, regardless of our beliefs or perspectives or actions or failures or mistakes or sins or opinions about whether God exists or not. I believe that God wants us each to flourish and thrive in this world here and now as we become more and more everything we can possibly be. In talking about the *for*ness of God, I want you to see how many of the dominant theological systems of thought that insist God is angry and hateful and just waiting to judge us unless we do or say or perform or believe the right things actually make people miserable and plague them with all kinds of new stresses and anxieties, never more so than when they actually start believing that God is really like that. I want you to see the radical, refreshing, revolutionary *for*ness that is at the heart of Jesus's message about God as it informs and transforms your entire life.

Then **ahead,** because when I talk about God, I'm not talking about a divine being who is behind, trying to drag us back to a primitive, barbaric, regressive, prescientific age when we believed Earth was flat and the center of the universe. I believe that God isn't backward-focused—opposed to reason, liberation, and progress—but instead is pulling us and calling us and drawing all of humanity forward—as God always has—into greater and greater peace, love, justice, connection, honesty, compassion, and joy. I want you to see how the God we see at work in the Bible is actually ahead of people, tribes, and cultures as God always has been. Far too many people in our world have come to see God as back there, primitive, not-that-intelligent, dragging everything backward to where it used to be. I don't understand God to be stuck back there, and I want you to experience this pull forward as a vital, active reality in your day-to-day life as you see just what God has been up to all along with every single one us.

All of which leads us to one more word to wrap it up: **so.** So what? So how do we live this? *So* is the question about what all this talking has to do with our everyday thinking and feeling and living.

To review, then:
Open,
Both,

With,
For,
Ahead,
and **So.**

One more note about notes: All of the places where I cite Scripture verses, as well as credits for other sources for information and suggestions for further reading, are included in the endnotes, organized there by theme or key phrases.

It's a fair bit of ground to cover, and my hope is that by the end you will say,

"Now *that's* what I'm talking about."

CHAPTER 2

OPEN

One time I was asked to speak to a group of atheists and I went and I had a blast. Afterward they invited me out for drinks, and we were laughing and telling stories and having all sorts of interesting conversation when a woman pulled me aside to ask me a question. She had a concerned look on her face and her brow was slightly furrowed as she looked me in the eyes and said, "You don't believe in miracles, do you?"

As I listened, I couldn't help but smile, because not long before that evening I'd been approached by a churchgoing, highly devout Christian woman who'd asked me, *with the exact same concerned look on her face, complete with furrowed brow,* "You believe in miracles, don't you?"

It's as if the one woman was concerned that I had lost my mind, while the other woman was concerned that I had lost my faith.

There's a giant either/or embedded in their questions, an either/or that reflects some of the great questions of our era:
Faith or intellect?
Belief or reason?
Miracles or logic?
God or science?

Can a person believe in things that violate all the laws of reason and logic and then claim to be reasonable and logical?

I point this either/or out because how we think about God is directly connected with how we think about the world we're living in.

When someone dismisses the supernatural and miraculous by saying, "Those things don't happen," and when someone else believes in something he can't prove and has no evidence for, those beliefs are both rooted in particular ways of understanding what kind of world we're living in and how we know what we know.

Often in these either/or discussions, people on both sides assume they're just being reasonable or logical or rational or something else intelligent-sounding, without realizing that the modern world has shaped and molded and formed how we think about the world, which leads to how we think about God, in a number of ways that are relatively new in human history and have a number of significant limits.

So before we talk about the God who is **with** us and **for** us and **ahead** of us, we'll talk about the kind of world we're living in and how that shapes how we know what we know.

First, we'll talk about the bigness of the universe,
then
the smallness of the universe,
then
we'll talk about you and what it is that makes you *you*,
and then
we'll talk about how all this affects how we understand and talk about God.

This will take a while—so stay with me—because the universe is way weirder than any of us ever imagined . . .

I. Welcome to the Red Shift

The universe,
it turns out,
is expanding.

Restaurant chains expand, waistbands expand, so do
balloons and those little foam animal toys that come in
pill-shaped capsules—but *universes*?

Or more precisely, *the* universe?
It's *expanding*?

Now the edge of the universe is roughly ninety billion
trillion miles away (*roughly* being the word you use when
your estimate could be off by A MILLION MILES), the
visible universe is a million million million million miles
across, and all of the galaxies in the universe are moving
away from all of the other galaxies in the universe at the
same time.

This is called *galactic dispersal,* and it may explain why
some children have a hard time sitting still.

The solar system that we live in, which fills less than a
trillionth of available space, is moving at 558 thousand
miles per hour. It's part of the Milky Way galaxy, and it
takes our solar system between 200 and 250 million
years to orbit the Milky Way *once.* The Milky Way
contains a number of smaller galaxies, including

the Fornax Dwarf,
the Canis Major,
the Ursa Minor,
the Draco,
the Leo I and the not-to-be-forgotten Leo II,
the Sculptor, and
the Sextans.
It's part of a group of fifty-four galaxies creatively called
the Local Group, which is a member of an even larger
group called the Virgo Supercluster (which had a number
of hit singles in the early eighties).

And happens to be traveling at 666 thousand miles an
hour.

(So be careful out there, and look both ways before you
cross the supernova.)

Back to our original question:
Expanding?

Around a hundred years ago, several astronomers,
among them Edwin Hubble, he of telescope fame, and
Vesto Slipher, he of awesome name fame, observed
distant galaxies giving off red light. Red is the color
galaxies emit when they're moving away from you, blue
when they're moving toward you—hence the term "red
shift."

Fast-forward to 1964, to two physicists working for the Bell Telephone Company, Arno Penzias and Robert Wilson. These men were unable to locate the source of strange radio waves they were continually picking up with their highly sensitive equipment. As they searched for the source of these waves, cleaned the bird droppings (which Penzias called "white dielectric material") off their instruments, and shared their findings with other scientists, they realized that they were picking up background radiation from a massive explosion.

An explosion, it's commonly believed, that happened a number of years ago—13.7 billion, to be more exact.

Apparently, before everything was anything, there was a point, called a *singularity,* and then there was a bang involving inconceivably high temperatures, loaded with enough energy and potential and possibility to eventually create what you and I know to be life, the universe, and everything in it.

The background radiation from this explosion, by the way, is still around in small amounts as the static on your television. (And you thought it was your cable company.)

Now when we get into sizes and distances and speeds this big and far and galactic and massive, things don't function in ways we're familiar with. For example, gravity.

Jump off the roof of your house, drop a plate on the floor in the kitchen, launch a paper airplane and you see gravity at work, pulling things toward our planet in fairly consistent and predictable ways. But in other places in the universe, gravity isn't so reliable. There are celestial bodies called *neutron stars* that have such strong gravity at work within them that they collapse in on themselves. These stars can weigh more than two hundred billion tons—more than all of the continents on Earth put together . . .
and fit in a teaspoon.

And then there's all that we don't know. A staggering 96 percent of the universe is made up of black holes, dark matter, and dark energy. These mysterious, hard to see, and even harder to understand phenomena are a major engine of life in the universe, leaving us with 4 percent of the universe that is actually knowable.

Which leads us to a corner of this 96 percent unknowable universe, to the outer edge of an average galaxy, to a planet called Earth. Our home.

Earth weighs about six billion trillion tons, is moving around the sun at roughly sixty-six thousand miles an hour, and is doing this while rotating at the equator at a little over a thousand miles an hour. So when you feel like your head is spinning, it is. Paris is, after all, going six hundred miles an hour.

Earth's surface is made up of about ten big plates and twenty smaller ones that never stop slipping and sliding, like Greenland, which moves half an inch a year. The general estimate is that this current configuration of continents that we know to be Africa, Asia, Europe, etc. has been like this about a tenth of 1 percent of history. The world, as we know it, is a relatively new arrangement.

Every day there are on average two earthquakes somewhere in the world that measure 2 or greater on the Richter scale, every second about one hundred lightning bolts hit the ground, and every nineteen seconds someone sitting in a restaurant somewhere hears Lionel Richie's song "Dancing on the Ceiling" one. more. time.

Speaking of time, here on Earth we travel around the sun every 365 days, which we call a year, and we spin once around every twenty-four hours, which we call a day. Our concepts of time, then, are shaped by large, physical, planetary objects moving around each other while turning themselves. Time is determined by physical space.

No planets, which are things,
no time.

We have calendars that divide time up into predictable, segmented, uniform units—hours and days and months and years. This organization into regular, sequential intervals that unfold with precise predictability has deeply shaped our thinking about time. These constructs are good and helpful in many ways—they help us get to our dentist appointments and remember each other's birthdays, but they also protect us from how elastic and stretchy time actually is.

If you place a clock on the ground and then you place a second clock on a tower, the hands of the clock on the tower will move faster than on the clock on the ground, because closer to the ground gravity is stronger, slowing down the hands of the clock.

If you stand outside on a starry night, the light you see from the stars is the stars as they were *when the light left them*. You are not seeing how those stars are now; you in the present are seeing how those stars *were* years and years and years *in the past*.

If you stand outside on a sunny day, you are enjoying the sun as it was *eight minutes ago.*

If you found yourself riding on a train that was traveling at the speed of light and you looked out the window, you would not see things ahead, things beside you, and things you had just passed. You would see everything *all at once*. You would lose your sense of past, present, and future because linear, sequential time would collapse into one giant NOW.

Time is not consistent:
it bends and warps and curves;

it speeds up and slows down;
it shifts and changes.
Time is relative, its consistency a persistent illusion.

It's an expanding,
shifting,
spinning,
turning,
rotating,
slipping and sliding universe we're living in.

There is no universal up;
there is no ultimate down;
there is no objective, stationary, unmoving place of rest
where you can observe all that ceaseless movement.

Sitting still,
after all,
is no different than maintaining a uniform approximate
constant state of motion.

There is no absolute viewpoint;
there are only views from a point.

Bendy, curvy, relative—**the past, present, and future are
illusions** as space-time warps and distorts in a stunning
variety of ways, leading us to another matter: matter.

The sun is both a star that we orbit,
and our primary source of energy.

It is a physical object,
and it is the engine of life for our planet.

The sun is made of matter,
and the sun is energy.
At the same time.

Albert Einstein was the first to name this, showing that matter is actually locked-up energy. And energy is liberated matter.

Perhaps you've seen posters of the Swiss patent clerk sticking his tongue out, with the wild hair and the rumors of how he was supposedly such a genius that he would forget to put his pants on in the morning. And then there's his famous $E = mc^2$ formula, which many of us could confidently write out on a chalkboard even if we couldn't begin to explain it.

Beyond all that, though, what exactly was it that he did?

What Einstein did, through his theories of general and special relativity, was show that the universe is way, way weirder than anyone had thought. I realize that *weirder* isn't the most scientific of terms, but Einstein's work took him from the bigness of the universe to the smallness of the universe, and that's when a string of truly stunning discoveries were made, discoveries that challenge our most basic ideas about the world we're living in.

II. Who Ordered That?

For thousands of years people have wondered what the universe is made of, assuming that there must be some kind of building block, a particle, a basic element, a cosmic Lego of sorts—something really small and stable that makes up everything we know to be everything. The possibilities are fascinating, because if you could discover this primal building material, you could answer countless questions about how we got here and what we're made of and where it's all headed . . .

You could, ideally, make sense of things.

Greek philosophers—among them Democritus, who lived twenty-five hundred years ago—speculated about this elemental building block, using a particular word for it. The Greeks had a word *tomos,* which referred to cutting or dividing something. Out of this they developed the concept of something that was *a-tomos,* something "indivisible, uncuttable," something that everything else was made of. Something really small, of which there is nothing smaller. Something *atomos,* from which we get the word *atom.*

Imagine what we'd learn if we could actually discover one of these atoms! That was the quest that compelled scientists and philosophers and thinkers for thousands of years until the late 1800s, when atoms were eventually discovered.

Atoms, it turns out, are small.

About one million atoms lined up side by side are as thick as a human hair.
A single grain of sand contains 22 quintillion atoms (that's 22 with 18 zeroes).

An atom is in size to a golf ball as a golf ball is in size to Earth.

That small.

But atoms, it was discovered, are made up of even smaller parts called *protons, neutrons,* and *electrons.* The protons and neutrons are in the center of the atom, called the *nucleus,* which is one-millionth of a billionth of the volume of the atom.

If an atom were blown up to the size of a stadium,
the nucleus would be the size of a grain of rice,
but it would weigh *more* than the stadium.

The discoveries continued as technology was developed to split those particles, which led to the discovery that those particles are actually made up of even smaller particles. And then technology was developed to split those particles and it was discovered that those particles are actually made up of even smaller particles. And then technology was developed to split *those* particles . . .

Down and down it went,
smaller and smaller,
further and further into the *sub*atomic world.

The British physicist J. J. Thomson discovered the
electron in 1897, which led to the discovery of an
astonishing number of new particles over the next few
years, from
bosons and
hadrons and
baryons and
neutrinos
to
mesons and
leptons and
pions and
hyperons and
taus.

Gluons were discovered, which hold particles together,
along with quarks, which come in a variety of types—
there are up quarks
and down quarks
and top quarks
and bottom quarks
and charmed quarks
and, of course,
strange quarks.

When an inconceivably small particle called a *muon* was identified, the legendary physicist Isaac Rabi is known for saying, "Who ordered that?"

By now somewhere around 150 subatomic particles have been identified, with new technology and research constantly emerging, the most impressive example of this happening at a facility known by the acronym CERN, which is near the Swiss–French border. Workers at CERN, an international collaboration of almost eight thousand scientists and several thousand employees, have built a sixteen-mile circular tunnel one hundred meters below Earth's surface called the Large Hadron Collider (LHC). At the LHC they fire two beams at each other, each with 3.5 trillion volts, hoping that in the ensuing collision particles will emerge that haven't been studied yet.

Physicists have talked with straight faces for years about how with this unprecedented level of energy and equipment and billions of dollars and the brightest scientific minds in the world working together they might be able to finally discover that incredibly important, terribly elusive particle called the . . .

Higgs Boson.

(Which they did. Go ahead, Google it. It's incredible. Even if it sounds like the name of a southern politician.)

Now, the staggeringly tiny size of atoms and subatomic particles is hard to get one's mind around, but it's what these particles *do* that forces us to confront our most basic assumptions about the universe.

Many popular images of an atom lead us to think that it's like a solar system, with the protons and neutrons in the center like the sun and the electrons orbiting in a path around the center as our planet orbits the sun.

But those early pioneering scientists learned that this is not how things actually are. What they learned is that electrons don't orbit the nucleus in a continuous and consistent manner; what they do is

disappear in one place and then appear in another place without traveling the distance in between.

Particles vanish and then show up somewhere else, leaping from one location to another, with no way to predict when or where they will come or go.

Niels Bohr was one of the first to come to terms with this strange new world that was being uncovered, calling these movements *quantum leaps.* Pioneering quantum physicists realized that **particles are constantly in motion, exploring all of the possible paths from point A to point B *at the same time.*** They're simultaneously everywhere and nowhere.

A given electron not only travels all of the possible routes from A to B, but it reveals which path it took *only when it's observed*. Electrons exist in what are called *ghost states,* exploring all of the possible routes they could take, until they are observed, at which point all of those possibilities *collapse* into the one they actually take.

Ever stood on a sidewalk in front of a store window and seen your reflection in the glass? You could see the items in the display window, but you could also see yourself, as if in a fuzzy mirror. Some of the light particles from the sun (called *photons*) went through the glass, illuminating whatever it was that caught your eye. Some of the particles from the sun didn't pass through the glass but essentially bounced off it, allowing you to see your reflection. Why did a certain particle go through the glass, and a certain other particle not?

It can't be predicted.

Some particles pass through the glass;
some don't.

You can determine possibilities,
you can list all kinds of potential outcomes,
but in the end, that's the best that can be done.

The physicist Werner Heisenberg was the first to name this disturbing truth about the quantum world: you can measure a particle's location, or you can measure its speed, but you can't measure both. Heisenberg's uncertainty principle, along with breakthroughs from Max Planck and many others, raised countless questions about the unpredictability of the universe on a small scale.

As more and more physicists spent more and more time observing the universe on this incredibly small scale, more truths began to emerge that we simply don't have categories for, an excellent example of this being the nature of light.

Light is the only constant, unchanging reality—all that curving and bending and shifting happens in contrast to light, which keeps its unflappable, steady course regardless of the conditions. But that doesn't mean it's free from some truly mind-bending behavior. Because things in nature are either waves or particles. There are dust particles and sound waves, waves in the ocean and particles of food caught in your friend's beard. That's been conventional wisdom for a number of years.

Particles and waves.
One or the other.
Particles are like bullets;
waves are spread out.
Particles can be only in specific locations;
waves can be everywhere.
Particles can't be divided; waves can.

But then there's light.

Light is made up of particles.
Light is a wave.

If you ask light a wave question, it responds as a wave.
Ask light a particle question, and it reveals itself to be
particles.
Two mutually exclusive things, things that have always
been understood to be either/or,
turned
out
to
be
both.
At the same time.

Niels Bohr was the first to name this, in 1926, calling it
complementarity.

Complementarity, the truth that something can be two
different things at the same time, leads us to another
phenomenon, one far more bizarre, called *entanglement*.

Communication as we understand it always involves a
signal of some sort—your voice, a telephone, a wire, a
radio wave, a frequency, a pulse—something to transmit
whatever it is from one place to another. Not so in the
subatomic realm, where particles consistently show that
they're communicating with one another *with no signal*

involved. Wolfgang Pauli identified this truly surreal property of subatomic particles in 1925 with his exclusion principle. Pairs of quantum particles, it was discovered, demonstrate an awareness of what the other is doing *after they've been separated.* Without any kind of signal.

The universe in its smallness presents us with a reality we simply don't have any frame of reference for:

A single electron can do forty-seven thousand laps around a four-mile tunnel—in one second.

Protons live ten thousand billion billion billion years, while muons generally live about two microseconds—and then they're gone.

If you're sitting in a chair that spins and I turn you around, I have to turn you 360 degrees to get you facing the same direction again. Electrons have been discovered that don't return to the front after being spun 360 degrees once; for that to happen you have to spin them *twice.*

Imagine playing tennis and discovering that sometimes you were able to hit the ball with your racquet, and other times the ball went *through* your racquet as if there were no webbing. You would immediately assume that there was some reason for this unexpected behavior of the ball and the racquet, and so you would work to figure out why this was happening. You'd take into account speed and force and the characteristics of the various materials: plastic and rubber and metal. All under the assumption that there was an explanation for the ball's action. You'd apply basic laws of physics and motion, and you'd think about similar circumstances involving similar speeds and sizes and shapes.

You'd be doing what scientists have been doing for a long time: operating under the assumption that the universe functions according to particular laws of motion *that can be known.*

But in the subatomic world,
things come and go,
disappear and appear,
spin and leap and communicate and demonstrate awareness of each other,
all without appearing to pay any attention to how the world is supposed to work.

Niels Bohr said that anyone who wasn't outraged on first hearing about quantum theory didn't understand what was being said.

It's important to pause here and make it clear that quantum theory is responsible for everything from X-rays and MRI machines and superconducting magnets, to lasers and fiber optics and the transistors that are the backbone of electronics, to computers. It's staggering just how many features of the modern world as we know it come from the contributions of quantum theory. The Nobel Laureate physicist Leon Lederman and the theoretical physicist Christopher Hill of Fermilab believe that quantum theory is arguably the most successful theory in the history of science.

———————

Which is all rather interesting, of course, but I'm assuming by now that you have a question, something along the lines of

What does any of this have to do with what we talk about when we talk about God?

Excellent question.

Three responses, then,
beginning with
energy,
and then moving to
involvement,
and then a bit about
surprise.

**Energy,
involvement,
surprise.**

Let's begin with your chair, because odds are that you're sitting in a chair while you read or listen to this book. It's probably made of metal or wood, foam, cloth, maybe leather. A few nuts and bolts, a screw or two, some paint, perhaps some nylon or plastic as well. If we were to take that wood or steel or cloth and put it under a high-powered microscope, we would see the basic elements and molecules and compounds that comprise those materials. And if we kept going, farther and farther into those basic materials, we would eventually be at the subatomic level, where we'd discover that the chair, like everything else in the universe, is made of atoms.

And atoms,
it turns out,
are 99.9 percent empty space.

If all of the empty space was taken out of all of the atoms in the universe, the universe would fit *in a sugar cube.*

An atom, in the end, is a thing. But a thing that is made up mostly of empty space, which is commonly believed to *not* be a thing. So what exactly are you sitting on?

A chair—a tangible, material, physical object—is made up of particles in motion, bouncing off each other, crashing into each other, coming in and out of existence billions of times in billionths of a second, existing in ghost states and then choosing particular paths for no particular, predictable reason.

Your chair appears to be solid,
but that solidity is a bit of an illusion.

It has weight and mass and shape and texture, and if
you don't see it in the dark and stub your toe on it, that
chair will cause your toe great pain, and yet your chair is
ultimately

a relationship of energy—

atoms bonded to each other in a particular way that
allows you to sit on that chair and be supported. Things
like chairs and tables and parking lots and planets may
appear to be solid, but they are at their core endless
frenetic movements of energy.

I talk about all of this red shifting and dark matter and
uncertainty and particle movement because most of us
were taught in science class that ours is a hard, stable,
tangible world that we can study and analyze because
it's there, right in front of us, and we can prove it in a lab.

Which is true.

But often another perspective came along as well,
the one that declared that there is a **clear distinction
between the material world and the immaterial world,
between the physical world and the spiritual world.**

**What we're learning from science,
however, is that that distinction isn't so clear after all.**

In other words, the line between
matter
and
spirit
may not be a line at all.

In an article about physicists searching for the Higgs Boson, Jeffrey Kluger writes in *TIME* magazine that they're "grappling with something bigger than mere physics, something that defies the mathematical and brushes up—at least fleetingly—against the spiritual."

Now obviously there are scientists who would bristle at any suggestion that this field of study has anything to do with the spiritual, pointing out that it's not mystical at all but very straightforward science, but for others, *brushing up against the spiritual* is a great way to put it because **the primary essence of reality is energy flow.** Things, no matter how great their mass is or how hard or solid or apparent their *thingness* is, are ultimately relationships of living energy.

This energy isn't destroyed or created—it simply changes form as it's conserved. If you're reading this book in printed form on paper and you were to burn it, the sum total of the book's energy would not change; it would simply go off and be other things than this book.

The amount of actual energy in the universe would stay the same.

And you wouldn't find out how the book ends.

Now, from *energy*,
let's move to *involvement*.

In the common view of the world most of us grew up with, there was a clear division between the subject and the object. Think of the stereotype of the objective scientist, standing cool and detached behind a glass wall, jotting observations onto a clipboard about whatever it is being studied. There is nothing wrong with this image; in fact, we owe this kind of thinking and practice a huge debt for the stunning array of technologies and inventions and luxuries we benefit from every day.

Somebody figured out how to fit a thousand songs in our pocket. Well done there.

But this image of detachment,
standing back at a distance,
watching and examining and analyzing things from a perceived place of *noninvolvement*, lives on in a number of ways that aren't true.

At the quantum level, to observe the atom is to affect it. The particle is a cloud of possibilities until it's observed, and then it chooses a particular path. The question you

ask light determines whether it will answer as a wave or a
particle.

In the view many have been taught,
the world is *out there,*
stationary and unmoved,
unaffected by us.
But in the quantum world,
observing *changes* things.

Matter is ultimately energy, and our interactions with
energy alter reality because we're involved, our world
an interconnected web of relationships with nothing
isolated, alone, or unaffected.

Even when there is an actual glass wall—
as helpful and accurate as traditional scientific
understandings are—
there is no glass wall in the end.

Central to the isolated, detached, common modern
worldview is the assumption that things exist in empty
space. Us outside, looking in. Studying, analyzing,
standing at a distance—observing the world that is *out
there in empty space.*

But the quantum world teaches us that space is—what's
the best word here?—*alive.* Particles can be found in
what appears to be empty space. The invisible substance

between us and the things and people around us actually contains something.

We are enmeshed in the world around us, not outside looking in, but inside looking . . . inside.

It's all energy,
and we're all involved.

These two truths,
the one about energy and the one about involvement,
lead us to a third truth, this one about surprise.

Your toaster doesn't do what it's supposed to. Seriously.

As things heat up, they register different colors, each new color representing an increase in temperature. And so, according to the standard assumptions about heat and corresponding color, your toaster should glow blue.

But it doesn't;
it glows red.

Why?
No one knows.

Which particle will pass through the glass in the shop window,
and which will reflect back? Where will that electron disappear, and when will it reappear—and where?

We can predict,
and we can identify patterns,
but at the most basic level,
we don't know.

The world surprises us.
And it surprises scientists too,
on a regular basis.

Energy,
involvement,
and
surprise.

I talk about all of this because when people object to the idea of God, to the idea that there is more beyond our tangible, provable-with-hard-evidence observations and experiences of the world, **they aren't taking the *entire* world into account.** A brief reading of modern science quite quickly takes us into all sorts of interesting and compelling places where the most intelligent, up-to-date, and informed scientists are constantly surprised by just how much *more* there is to the universe.

III. You Dirty Star, You

Which leads us to you,
right there in the middle of it all.

Actually, we *are* in the middle of it all, with a human being
(roughly a meter tall on average, kids included) halfway
between the largest size we can comprehend, the width
of the known universe, and the smallest size discovered
thus far in the universe.

And you,
you are fascinating.

You lose fifty to a hundred and fifty strands of hair a day,
you shed ten billion flakes of skin a day,
every twenty-eight days you get completely new skin,
and every nine years your entire body is renewed.

(This dead skin we shed makes up 90 percent of
household dust. So feel free to vacuum more.)

And yet your body, in the midst of this relentless
shedding and dying and changing and renewing,
continues to remember to be you,
strand by strand,
flake by flake,
atom by atom.

Your body is made up of around seventy-five trillion cells, every one of those cells containing hundreds of thousands of molecules with six feet of DNA in every cell containing over three billion letters of coding. These cells are a potent blend of matter and memory—bones and hair and blood and teeth and at the same time personality and essence and predispositions and habits.

You are an exotic combination of matter and memory, with a fine line in between.

Millions of cells, drifting through the universe, assembled and configured and finely tuned at this second to be you, but inevitably moving on in the next seconds to be other things and other people.

The atoms that make you *you* in this very second may have earlier been part of a stork,
or Mars,
or a mushroom,
or a squid,
or a coconut,
or Ohio,
or Buddha,
or Cher.

Imagine that your uncle died and in his will he left you his beloved old wooden boat. You love your uncle and out of respect for him you decide that you're going to fix up his old boat, making it good as new. And so you start with the hull, replacing the old boards with new ones. But as you work rebuilding the hull, you realize that the deck needs replacing as well. And so the next year, you remove all of the boards on the deck and replace them with new ones, plank by plank, until the boat has an entirely new deck. But spending all that time working on the deck convinces you that the hardware isn't reliable; you're not sure which pieces would work if you were to actually launch the boat, and which would snap with the slightest strain. And so you set out to replace all of the hardware. . . . If you keep this up, at some point you will have replaced the entire boat, **and yet when you take your friends out for a ride, you will tell them that *this* is the boat your uncle left you in his will.**

The enduring reality of the boat, then, is in the pattern, not the planks.

The planks come and go, but the pattern remains. *You* are a pattern, moving through time, constantly changing and yet precisely consistent. Some have said we're like "light at the end of a spinning stick."

The basic elements of life are actually quite common— hydrogen, carbon, nitrogen, oxygen, and a few others. The dirt below us, the sky above us, the sun, moon, and stars, we're all made of the same stuff.

You share over 60 percent of your genes with fruit flies, you share over 90 percent of your genes with mice, and you share 96 percent of your DNA with the large apes.

So when you read about aging singers or actors or politicians who *used to be* stars—well yes, of course they were . . . we *all* used to be stars.

One of my sons recently had a loose tooth that was driving him crazy. He'd sit at the table while we ate dinner, hand in his mouth, moving the tooth back and forth, trying to loosen it enough for it to come out. Day after day, talking about it and fussing with it and telling us just how badly he wanted it to come out. And then it came out—while we were at the beach. He started jumping up and down in the sand, celebrating, doing one of those dances that only an eleven-year-old boy can do, hoisting his now-removed tooth above his head, victorious.

He then turned to me and asked: If he threw it in the ocean, would he still get something from the tooth fairy? I said yes, feeling free to speak on behalf of the tooth fairy, who happened to be sitting next to me in a swimsuit.

And so he ran up to the waterline,
cocked his arm back,
and threw his tooth into the ocean.

I tell you this story because at some point today you will eat. You will eat for several reasons, chief among them being survival. If you don't eat, you die, because your body needs food. And food comes from the earth. It's planted, watered, cultivated, exposed to the sun, and then harvested, transported, prepared, and placed on your plate. Between the sun and the rain and the nutrients in the soil, that food received what it needed to keep you alive.

At least for a while. Because at some point, you will die.

Your body will then be buried in the earth, where it will gradually decompose until it fully returns to the soil, the same soil that provided the nutrients for the food to grow that kept you alive . . .

Your body, which is 65 percent water,
comes from the earth,
is sustained by the earth,
and will return to the earth.

The impulse, then, to throw one's tooth into the ocean is quite sensible, not to mention poetic.

We're made of dust and we come from the stars,
we're both skin and soul,
blood and being—
at 98.6 degrees continually radiating about 100 watts of energy into our surroundings, containing 7×10^{18} joules

of potential energy, the equivalent of 30 large hydrogen bombs.

I talk about you like this because **when I'm talking about you, I'm talking about the paradox at the core of our humanity—that we're made of dust and stars and energy and patterns of planks and yet, as it's written in the Psalms, we've been *crowned with glory and honor.***

We are both large and small,
strong and weak,
formidable and faint,
reflecting the image of the divine,
and formed from dust.

We get stuck in traffic one day and find ourselves cursing within seconds, while another time we sit with a friend who's dying of cancer and are filled with an ocean of compassion.

The slightest barbed word from a coworker can cause our blood to boil, and yet as a friend comes down the aisle at her wedding our heart feels like it's a thousand miles wide.

We can easily find the most basic disciplines incredibly challenging, making us feel impotent and devoid of willpower, and yet we walk through a building designed by a master architect, taking in the light coming through the glass and the way the space is laid out, and we find ourselves asking over and over again, "How did someone think this up and then actually see it through to completion?"

We're an exotic blend of
awesome
and
pathetic,
extraordinary
and
lame,
big
and
small.

We hear about people climbing Mount Everest *blind,*
and we hear about serial killers opening fire in a crowded theater,
and we're still surprised,
because we're still asking the same old question:
What are we made of?

The answer,
of course,
is atoms.

You're made of trillions of atoms.

Those trillions of atoms form molecules,
those molecules form cells,

those cells form systems—
nervous, immune, limbic, circulatory, digestive, muscular,
respiratory, skeletal, to name a few—
and those systems eventually form a far larger,
more complicated system which we know to be
you.

This arrangement that makes you *you* results from
something called **hierarchy,** in which each component
is joined to other similar components to form together
something new that is more complex.

There are more atoms than molecules,
but a molecule is more complex than an atom.
There are more molecules than cells,
but a cell is more complex than a molecule.
And so on up the hierarchy it goes, with increasingly
complex levels of organization at each higher level.

Each higher level, then, is smaller in number, but greater
in complexity. Smaller in breadth, but greater in depth.

From
trillions of atoms
to
one you.

These trillions of atoms are incessantly coming and
going, billions of times a second, all of them knowing
their place within the hierarchy that is you, and yet every

single one of those atoms is able at any second to cease being you and join another hierarchy, taking its place in making someone or something else.

This truth about hierarchy and parts leads us to something called *holism*.

To explain holism, imagine the best scientists in the world, taking you apart, bone by bone, cell by cell, atom by atom

—well, maybe not. That's fairly gruesome, isn't it?

Let's try coming at this from a different angle: There's a good chance you have an elbow, probably even two. It's *your* elbow, and yet where would we find *you* in *your elbow*? An elbow is made of skin and bones and blood and tendons, all of those basic elements made of even more basic elements that are ultimately made of atoms that are constantly coming to and going from you, leaving to make other people and things and places and maybe even other elbows on other people.

All of it raising the question:
So where are *you* in your body?

Your body could be taken apart all the way down to the last atom, and yet we would never begin to locate the unique essence that we know to be you. A bone is a bone is a bone; same with an eye or a tooth or large ears that stick out. They're each made of the same material that everything else is made of. At the same time, though, if they belong to you, they are uniquely yours.

This is because there are dimensions to you that transcend the actual parts and pieces that you refer to as your body—qualities and characteristics that emerge only at a larger, collective level, when all those parts are assembled to form you. **Holism is the reality that emerges only when all the parts are put together but can't be individually located, labeled, or identified at a smaller, component, parts level.**

Hierarchy is about parts, and your body is made of lots of them—
206 bones,
proteins that run into each other a billion times a second,
enzymes that do a thousand jobs a second,
a brain with one hundred billion interconnected neurons,
each neuron having ten thousand connections and synapses—
and yet you are more than the sum of your parts in the same way that

novels are more than just the words,
songs are more than just the notes,
and boats are more than just the planks.

Holism is when two plus two equals infinity.

Holism is the truth that your consciousness and personality and awareness cannot be located in your physicality, in the same way that your identity and thoughts and fears and favorite ice cream and opinions about Jim Carrey movies can't be detected in your elbow or your nose or your pancreas.

Holism is your awareness that you cannot hold *soul* in your hand.

Holism is the living, breathing truth that you-the-whole are more than the sum of your parts.

Holism is the mystery at the heart of your existence—the fact that whatever it is that makes you most uniquely *you* cannot be measured or assessed or even found in any conventional, rational, scientific way.

Holism is your sense that there's more going on here, even though it can't be located in any one person, thing, or event.

These truths about the holism that is each of us leads us to a larger holism, one that continues to unfold across and outside of time itself.

Think back hundreds of millions of years ago to the most primitive life-forms that existed long before any humans roamed Earth and made fires and hung fuzzy dice from their rearview mirrors.

Were primordial bacteria discussing where they came
from?
Were single-celled heterotrophs singing songs about
love?
Were dinosaurs writing poems about their desire to make
a difference in the world?

No, they weren't. They weren't because dinosaurs
weren't aware that they were dinosaurs, and algae and
bacteria and trees and swamps didn't have thoughts, and
fish didn't wonder why bad things happen to good fish.

Obvious, but astonishing.

**Consciousness didn't come until later in creation, with
the arrival of humans,** and probably not even in humans
until relatively recently in history.

Alphabets and written language and poetry and
reflection and organized societies and laws and Oprah's
book club and all of the things that make up civilization
and thought and culture came much, much later in
human history.

**You are aware that you are you, which is a phenomenon
that simply didn't exist here for billions of years.**

There is a movement forward, toward greater and greater
awareness and consciousness and connectivity, that has
been unfolding across the history of the universe, an

ever-expanding enlightening that transcends any one of us, all cultures, and humanity as a whole. A massive and epic holism that continues to increase in complexity and depth and dimension to this very day.

———————

So why all this talk about hierarchy and holism?

Because often people have a hard time believing there's a God because we can't see God, we don't have hard evidence for the existence of God, and we don't have any proof we can study or analyze or evaluate in any scientific, tangible way.

The twist on all of this is that we all agree you exist. You, your elbows and pancreas and sternum are tangible and able to be measured and evaluated in very straightforward ways, but your soul? That's a bit more difficult to capture. Let alone measure or study.

And yet we all agree that there's more to you than your physical body.

It's been said that the soul is naked of all things that bear names.

A bit like God, because when I'm talking about God, I'm talking about a reality known, felt, and experienced, but one that cannot be located in any specific physical space in any tangible way.

When we talk about God, then, we're talking about something very real and yet beyond our conventional means of analysis and description.

The Germans, interestingly enough, have a word for this: they call it *grenzbegrifflich*.

Grenzbegrifflich describes that which is very real but is beyond analysis and description. When I'm talking about God, I'm talking about your intuitive sense that reality at its deepest flows from the God who is *grenzbegriff*.

To explain more about what *grenzbegrifflich* means, I need to talk about what happened when I went skateboarding in North Carolina twenty years ago.

IV. The Sea We're Swimming In

I was visiting my friend Ian in Charlotte, and late one night he took me skateboarding all over the city, showing me his favorite spots and embankments and parks.

One of the places he took me was a flat, open concrete space that sank down into a large bowl at one end. He went first, building up speed and then dropping down into the bowl and skating around the inner rim. I quickly followed him. (Note to self: skateboarding in the dark in an unfamiliar city in spots you haven't skated before isn't always the smartest thing to do.)

I was going faster and faster as I got closer to the edge of the bowl—which I didn't reach, at least on my board. What I learned is that this open space used to be a parking lot, and when they removed those cement curbs that you nudge your front tires up to, they didn't remove one of the embedded iron bars used to hold the curb in place. Three inches of iron bar, a half-inch wide, sticking up out of the concrete. In the dark. Just enough to bring my board to an instant halt, launching me Superman style out and above and then down into the bowl—nine, eight, seven, six feet to the concrete below.

It was the kind of thing fifteen-year-old boys discover on YouTube and play over and over and over again, laughing hysterically at the guy who got launched into the bowl.

And yes, there was lots of blood.

Now, as I tell you that story you aren't surprised—about the physics part of it, that is—because in high school we were all taught that (everybody together now) *an object in motion stays in motion unless acted on by an outside force*.

We know this because in science class we learned what's called a *classical view* of the world, based on Isaac Newton's mechanical laws of physics. These laws are so basic to our thinking about speed and motion and mass and movement that it's hard for us to comprehend just how revolutionary they were when Newton's groundbreaking book *Principia* was first published in 1687. At that time, the reason the majority of people would have given as to why the world works the way it does is because, well, *God made it that way*.

That's just how things are; why would you need an explanation beyond that?

But Newton, Newton didn't see it that way. Newton insisted that there were predictable, knowable, rational rules and explanations that govern how the universe operates, causes that lead to effects, and clear connections between the two.

(If a man is traveling at a certain speed in a certain direction, and he has a certain mass and there is a certain amount of friction involved, and an opposing force interrupts that particular motion, the man will travel a particular distance through the air before making contact, face, knees, and wrists first, with the concrete at a certain speed with a certain amount of impact force— and a certain amount of blood.)

Newton showed that you could know the speed *and* position of something because *motion was understood to be continuous and consistent*. Given enough data about weight and speed and a number of other variables, outcomes could be computed and accurately predicted. This new worldview brought with it all kinds of exciting possibilities. Things could be built, engineered, created, and designed by plotting trajectories and paths and measuring how much opposing force would be needed to stop and move and push and pull things of certain weights and certain speeds.

As more and more natural explanations were discovered for why things are the way they are, the idea of a clock, with its precise measurements and enduring consistency, replaced the actions of the gods as the primary way people began to understand how the universe functions. Cogs and wheels and buttons and pulleys became popular images—with all of the parts working together like an efficient, well-calibrated machine.

A new way to see the world arose, one governed by precise regularity—
orderly,
exact,
predictable.

Along with these new ways of conceiving the physical world came new ways of thinking about *how* we know what we know. We've all heard the phrase "I think, therefore I am" from René Descartes. It's so familiar that it's easy to lose the sense of how groundbreaking it was when he first said it, because for the majority of people at that time knowledge was seen as something that humans were given by God through what's called *revelation*. If you asked how we know what we know, the standard answer was, "God told us." But Descartes didn't see it that way. He insisted that we can know what we know not because a divine being chose for some reason to reveal it to us but because we arrived at that knowledge through our own reason and logic. Now obviously this wasn't the first time anyone used logic or reason, but as his idea caught on, it was new to have that many people across that wide an array of disciplines and pursuits embracing such a new understanding of how we know what we know.

That era, called the Golden Age of Certainty, gave birth to what we call the scientific method—the testing and poking and prodding and experimenting and examining of evidence, the running of multiple tests, the comparing of data from one trial to another. Instead of humans as passive recipients of knowledge the gods decided to give them, the image of the scientist emerged, standing over the subject, detached and objective, actively making precise observations and arriving at valid conclusions.

This explosion of discovery and exploration, also called the Enlightenment, moved human history forward in an astonishing number of new ways, out of the Dark Ages and medieval world and into a new era of staggering technologies and knowledge and breakthroughs.

This Enlightenment leap—this good and needed leap— handed us a number of ways of understanding the world that have worked on us and influenced us for several hundred years now in positive ways. But these understandings also have limits, limits that we become acutely aware of when we talk about God.

Let's look briefly at two of these limits and how they've deeply shaped the beliefs and practices of our modern world before we move on.

First, a limit that affects how we filter knowledge.

As reason and logic became more and more prominent, **other ways of knowing became less emphasized.** If the only way we know things is through the testing and poking and prodding of the scientific method, what happens when we know something in a way that bypasses those particular tests and processes? Does *everything* you know have to be able to be proven intellectually?

In the lab, for something to be valid it has to be proven repeatably and repeatedly through multiple tests and experiments. There has to be demonstrable evidence. But what about those things that you absolutely, positively know to be true but would be hard-pressed to produce evidence for if asked?

Explain how that particular song moves you.
Articulate why you fell in love with *that* person.
Provide data for the manner in which that meal with those friends made your soul soar.

Most of the things in life we're most sure of, many of those events and experiences that are more real to us than anything else, lots of sensations we have no doubt actually happened—these are things we cannot prove with any degree of scientific validity.

Which leads us to a crucial truth: there are other ways of knowing than only those of the intellect.

In the lab, we can stand objectively over the subject, testing and retesting and examining, filtering the data through the lens of rational repeatability.

But outside the lab,
in the course of our very real lives,
some experiences *act on us*.
We engage with them passively as they happen to us.

They seize us and capture us and woo us and abduct us.
We don't stand over *them;*

they jump *us* in a dark alley and pin us to the ground and won't let us go.

We are way too complex,
and so is the world—
too much surprise,
too many possibilities,
too much that defies our limited logical categories—
to fit everything through the narrow filter of reason alone.

We're like fish, swimming in the rational waters of the Enlightenment, disconnected from a number of other ways we know and feel and experience. We've been swimming in this sea, enjoying it and benefiting from it, but slowly realizing that it hasn't been totally good for us. The intellect has a way of building a fence around the heart, cutting us off from what we know to be true in a way that is hard to prove *according to the categories in which proof matters*. In the Enlightenment sea we learned how to grasp, how to control, how to master whatever it is we're studying. We've stood behind the glass wall and made the appropriate observations.

But we've been around for only .0001 percent of Earth's history, 97 percent of Earth's species still haven't been discovered, and all of the bones we've dug up from our earliest ancestors could fit in the back of a pickup. We're simply not the masters we've been told we are.

In the words of Soren Solari, who has a PhD in integrative neuroscience, "It's fun to speculate about exactly what's going on in our brains when we surf, but the reality today is that we don't know."

Second, from narrow filters, let's turn to a limit that's been working on us over the past several hundred years, this one about parts and wholes.

Imagine how earth-shattering it was for people to learn that the sun does not revolve around Earth or that volcanoes erupt for reasons other than divine anger or that canyons were formed by natural causes rather than the work of really, really large hands or that our planet is not resting on turtles all the way down. Mind-blowing. As more and more rational, logical explanations were given for how the natural world works, the previous supernatural, magical, and mythical explanations became more and more irrelevant. It turned out that lots of phenomena weren't as mysterious as everybody had assumed they were for thousands of years. This burgeoning scientific knowledge led to the growing question, If *this* can be explained in a very straightforward, logical way, can *that*? Or *that*? Or *that*? What's to say that, given enough time, we won't figure it *all* out?

These questions led to even bigger questions, which turned into assumptions, which eventually evolved into beliefs, all beginning with the question:

Can everything ultimately be explained without any supernatural, magical/mythical, *divine* causes?

As these questions and assumptions have worked on us and influenced us for several hundred years, they've led to the belief among lots and lots of educated, intelligent people that *given enough time, we'll arrive at explanations for everything.* Whatever it is that is a mystery to us now, given enough time we'll be able to reduce it to its parts and understand it through very straightforward, rational, logical explanations.

And that belief rests on an even deeper faith—a really, really significant one: if everything can be explained without any outside, supernatural, or divine factors, then the universe is ultimately the sum of its parts.

This belief system is based on *reduction,* and it holds tightly to the faith that given enough time we'll have all the answers, and mystery, like Elvis, will have left the building.

Get whatever it is down to its tiniest pieces,
and you'll get whatever answers you're looking for . . .
because, in the end,
things are what they are,
no more,
and no less.

Newton's work pointed to a rational, reductionistic world, one where there are causes that lead to predictable results. A world where matter is stable and consistent, all of the independent parts functioning together to form the whole.

A world where all there is is, in the end, all there is.

But when I'm talking about God, I'm talking about the divine being who can't be located tangibly with the kind of evidence that the rationalism of reductionism demands in the same way that you cannot be located in your eyelashes or spine or shoulder.

Which takes us back to faith, because when someone says that we don't understand something fully right now but we will given enough time, that is, of course, a belief. That's faith. We aren't at that point talking about people of faith versus people of science; we're talking about *all* people of faith, just faith in different things.

Once again, we're like fish, swimming in the sea of the Enlightenment, benefiting greatly from endless advancements and yet limited at times by the narrow filters of the intellect and the diminishing reductionism that insists this is all there is.

Speaking of fish, this leads us to another dimension of the God who is *grenzbegriff,* a dimension involving lots of bumper stickers.

Have you seen that sticker some Christians put on their cars, the one shaped like a fish? That comes from a first-century tradition of Christians carving or painting the faith symbol somewhere on their home or business to let others know that they were followers of Jesus. Great. But then others, in response to this sticker, put another sticker on their bumper, this one the same shape as the fish sticker, but with legs and a tail and (in the middle of the fish) the word "evolve." Nice. This sticker is about evolution, which the owner of the car mistakenly sees as something that is *fundamentally against* the Jesus sticker. I've actually seen car bumpers with the *evolve* sticker upside down with the Jesus sticker on top of it—a sort of "Oh yeah, two can play that game" gesture.

And so the battle of the bumpers goes on,
all of it a massive exercise in missing the point.

The point being hierarchy and holism.

Fossil evidence and carbon dating and exploration and discovery are central to the endless human desire for answers. New theories arise; they're proven, tweaked, adjusted; and sometimes a better theory comes along to replace one that has proven holes in it—that's the scientific process. It's magnificent at lower levels of hierarchy, helping us understand neurons and rocks and oceans and species.

But it fails at higher levels of hierarchy when we encounter holism.

Science does an excellent job of telling me why I don't have a tail, but it can't explain why I find that interesting.

Science shines when dealing with parts and pieces, but it doesn't do all that well with *soul*.

It can do a brilliant job of explaining how we and other species have adapted and evolved, but it falls short when it comes to where the reverence humming within us comes from.

When I'm talking about God, I'm talking about the *grenzbegriff* kind of faith that sees science and faith as the dance partners they've always been, each guiding and informing the other, bringing much-needed information and insight to their respective levels of hierarchy. To see them at odds with each other is to confuse the levels of hierarchy, resulting in all sorts of needless debates, misunderstandings, and terrible bumper stickers.

I say all of this about science and faith because when I'm talking about God, I'm talking about the source of *all* truth, whatever labels it wears, whoever says it, and wherever it's found—from a lab to a cathedral to a pub to Mars.

This is important, because for many in our world,
somewhere along the way reality got divided up into the
secular and the sacred,
the religious and the regular,
the holy and the common—
the understanding being that you're talking about *either*
one
or
the other
but not *both*
at the same time.

This dis-integrated understanding of reality—
the one that puts God on one side and not the other,
the one that divides the world up into two realms—
it's lethal, and it cuts us off from the depths and
separates us from the source.

Because sometimes you need a biologist,
and sometimes you need a poet.
Sometimes you need a scientist,
and sometimes you need a song.

———————

So, there's a bit about you and the universe, and the God
who is *grenzbegriff.* Now, to wrap this chapter up, let's
go to Boston.

A few years ago I was speaking in that fine city, and
afterward a woman told me about the time she had

been in the hospital for ongoing cancer treatment, lying in bed thinking that she wasn't going to make it. She remembers being lower than she'd ever been before, filled with despair, wondering if she was going to die soon, when the night-shift nurse entered her room and began to lovingly care for her. Throughout the night the nurse returned repeatedly, checking on her and calming her and reassuring her and speaking to her in a way that lifted her entire being and gave her hope. In the morning, she woke up feeling like a different person. She then asked the morning nurse for the name of the woman who had been caring for her, giving a detailed description.

The nurse said that no one who fit that description worked on that floor of the hospital, not to mention the night before in this woman's room.

What do you do with that story?

As a pastor, I've heard countless stories like this one over the years. People sitting at their kitchen table, realizing that they don't have enough money to buy groceries, when the doorbell rings and they open the door to find their front porch filled with bags of food. Really strange, odd, surreal sorts of stories. Some of them can be attributed to basic coincidence, but over the years I've heard tons of them—and not just from really zealous religious people who carry large Bibles with their names engraved on the covers, but also from educated, somewhat cynical people with PhDs who own companies and have expertise in fields so technical I barely understand what it is they do all day.

Now some people hear a story about the woman in the hospital and immediately say, "Yes, of course! That was an angel taking care of her! They're all around us, watching over us and guiding us and protecting us," and then they proceed to quote verses from the Bible while telling *their* angel stories.

Others hear people responding like this and roll their eyes, dismissing it all as crazy talk that belongs in the same category as talk of demons and spirits and blind people suddenly seeing. They are quick to point out that no one has any proof of such things and that it's superstitious ideas like these from earlier, mythological religion that, if left unchecked, lead to wars and ignorance and all sorts of really bad religious shows on cable television.

One says, "Of *course* she was an angel!"
The other says, equally emphatically, "Angels don't exist!"

I'll never forget the conversation I had with a brilliant, well-known woman about the resurrection of Jesus, which she dismissed as fantasy along with "all of those beliefs in things that don't happen." She speaks for untold masses who check out as soon as the discussion turns to people being swallowed by fish and walking on water and, of course, rising from the dead.

There is, however, a problem with decisively dismissing all miracles out of hand, and that problem is subatomic particles, which, we've learned, disappear in one place and appear in another place *without traveling the distance in between.* Strange things *do happen,* things with no precedent and no explanation, every single day and every single moment, billions and billions of times a second, all around us, in our bodies. Time is bendy and curvy and not consistent, the universe is curved, and if Earth were slightly closer to the sun we'd all cook and if it were slightly farther away we'd all freeze.

It's all—let's use a very specific word here—*miraculous.* You, me, love, quarks, sex, chocolate, the speed of light— it's all miraculous, and it always has been.

When people argue for the existence of a supernatural God who is somewhere else and reaches in on occasion to do a miracle or two, they're skipping over the very world that surrounds us and courses through our veins and lights up the sky right here, right now.

We live in a very, very weird universe. One that is roughly 96 percent unknown.

I tell you this story about the woman in the hospital because when I talk about the God who is *grenzbegriff,* I'm talking about the kind of intellectually honest faith that is open-minded enough to admit that some phenomena have no rational explanation.

To be closed-minded to anything that does not fit within predetermined and agreed-upon categories is to deny our very real experiences of the world. We're here, this is real, subatomic particles travel all possible paths and then choose one when observed, and there is no precedent for such a thing. This is not avoiding important things like evidence and proof and logic; this is the tacit acknowledgment that some events, experiences, and truths simply exist outside of those particular categories.

Which leads to one last thought, one about being open-minded. In our world today, we often hear people talk about being open-minded and about how religion can be stifling because of how *closed-minded* it can be.

Now it's true that religion can lead people to be incredibly closed-minded, but the terms *open-minded* and *closed-minded* aren't usually applied accurately. To believe that this is all there is and we are simply collections of neurons and atoms—that's being closed to anything beyond that particular size and scope of reality.

But to believe that there's more going on here, that there may be reality beyond what we can comprehend—that's something else.

That's being open.

CHAPTER 3

BOTH

Now that we've explored a bit about the kind of universe we're living in and how we think about thinking about how we know what we know, we'll talk just for a bit about *how* we talk when we talk about God.

Have you ever heard someone confidently asserting this or that about God down to the most striking and exact detail and thought, "Who is this person to know that?" Or maybe it was the opposite—have you ever heard someone going on and on with great conviction about how it's all just a giant cosmic hairball and how could any human ever claim to actually know anything about God?

In the one case, it was the speaker's certainty that was unnerving;
in the other case, it was too much ambiguity that didn't sit well with you.

But in both cases, what we see is the importance of understanding that there's *what* you're saying, and then there's *how* you're saying it . . .

———————

Let's say that you work in a large office, and one day you come back from lunch and there's a group of people gathered around the cubicle three down from yours, which belongs to Sheila from accounts payable. You wander over and learn that Sheila's boyfriend Simon has just proposed to her during a picnic lunch in a nearby park and she said yes. Everybody is happy for Sheila and they're taking turns examining her ring and Sheila can't stop smiling, and so you ask her, "Sheila, tell us about Simon."

And so Sheila starts in: "Well, he's five-foot-ten, he drives a Toyota, he wears size nine and a half shoes, and he was born in Kentucky and he's left-handed and he's in a Tuesday night bowling league and he doesn't like mayonnaise . . ."

At some point while Sheila is telling you about Simon you probably think to yourself, "This is strange."

You think this not because Sheila is lying or avoiding the question or distorting the truth, but precisely because she is *telling the truth* about Simon, things that can be objectively proven to be true. It's just that women who have gotten engaged an hour earlier don't usually feel the need to tell you whether or not their man likes mayonnaise.

Or let's say your car is making a loud ticking noise and so you take it to the repair shop. A mechanic looks under the hood, takes it for a drive around the block, and then comes out to the waiting room and tells you that the car "is in a bad mood—it's clearly got some issues it needs to work out."

This is not helpful, because you want to know exactly what is wrong with the car, exactly what replacement parts are needed, how long it will take to fix it, and how much it's going to cost.

Or let's say you're having open-heart surgery, lying there on the table with your rib cage spread open, and you hear the surgeon say to one of the nurses, "Hey, gimme one of those scalpels over there—how about a feisty one with some attitude?"

Aside from the obvious question, "You're *awake* during open-heart surgery?" why would it disturb you to hear the doctor talk like this? Because you want to know that the surgeon knows exactly what scalpel she needs to do the work; you want to hear her ask for the "RQ8F7 double-edged Incisotron" or something like that.

There are, it's important to note, different kinds of language.

There is technical, precise language, the kind that surgeons and car mechanics use to be as objective as possible in naming exactly what is wrong, describing precisely what is needed, or accurately listing steps and procedures with great care and definition, as in this online discussion about transistor modules:

> The part marked K2313 is a metal-oxide-semiconductor field-effect transistor[;] . . . a voltage on the oxide-insulated gate electrode can induce a conducting channel between the two other contacts called source and drain. It is a Toshiba 2SK2313 . . .

Clear, unambiguous, with as little as possible that could lead somebody to think you were talking about something else. We use language like this in thousands of ways every day because without it, we wouldn't get the right doses of medicine, planes couldn't take off and land, and we wouldn't know which transistor module to use.

But when Sheila's going on about Simon, telling you facts and truths and being quite precise about exactly how tall he is and where he was born, something doesn't feel right, because you were expecting Sheila to say something less technical and factual and literal and more figurative and poetic—something like, "I feel like I finally found my other half."

Technical language has limits. It can describe some things very well, but in other situations, like love, it falls flat. It's inadequate. It fails.

When we're betrayed, we say it feels like we've been kicked in the stomach.

When our child takes her first steps, we say that we're over the moon.

When the DJ plays just the right music, we say she blew the roof off the place.

Now the truth is, we weren't kicked in the stomach. We aren't over the moon; we're right here. And the roof is still firmly on the building.

Intense experiences and extreme situations—
like great pain and anguish,
or unspeakable joy and ecstasy—
need extreme, large, giantesque language because other kinds of words and phrases aren't enough.

Language is flexible, fluid, able to twist and morph in vast and varied ways. There are rants and poems and metaphors and parodies and stories and fables and analogies and similes and haiku (remember those?) and instruction manuals and palindromes . . .
When Jay-Z raps,

> I'm not a businessman,
> I'm a business, man

he's doing something really powerful *with a comma,* using it to evoke meaning and history and power. And it's funny.

All with two lines that are virtually identical.

When that old song begins,

> Sometimes I feel like a motherless child . . .

we all know that to be alive, you have to have been born from an actual mother. But there is a pain that comes from having a mother but not having a mother, the haunting ache of abandonment, the feeling of distance from the primal, nurturing embrace we know to be "mom."

All that, in the first line of the song.

When George Mallory was asked why he climbed Mt. Everest, he replied, "Because it's there."

Language soars and dips and sometimes gets right to the point and other times goes on and on and on with flourish and flair. Sometimes it describes accurately and completely complex and detailed concepts and mechanisms and processes, and other times language just isn't enough.

Recently my family and I were in the car when a friend called to tell us that the father of one of my son's friends had just killed himself. Every day for three years I'd seen that dad when I picked my kids up after school; we'd talked in the parking lot and on the sidelines of the football field and in our front yards countless times. And then he was gone.

Sometimes there aren't words.
Sometimes sentences and phrases can't do the moment justice.
Sometimes language fails,
and you're speechless.

So when we talk about God we're using language, language that employs a vast array of words and phrases and forms to describe a reality that is fundamentally *beyond* words and phrases and forms.

In the biblical book of Exodus, Moses is told to hide along a section of rock because God is going to pass by and Moses is going to get to see God's *back*. In one ancient commentary on this story, the best Moses gets is a glimpse of *where God just was*. This same Moses reminds the Hebrews that when they experienced God, they "saw no form of any kind." In the New Testament it's written that God is the one "who dwells in unapproachable light, whom no one has seen or can see."

There are limits to certainty because God, it's repeated again and again, is spirit. And spirit has no shape or form. Spirit, Jesus said, is like the wind. It comes and goes and blows where it pleases.

Words and images point us to God;
they help us understand the divine,
but they are not God.

For example, gender.

In the ancient world, it was observed that a woman became pregnant only when she'd been with a man. It was assumed, then, based on primitive, limited understandings of biology, that the man's contribution must be the essence of the life force and a woman's the place where that life force was carried and held and nurtured. God, it was believed, was the life force of the world, so God must be like a father.

Or take early agricultural settings, where women used hoes to break up the ground for planting. Women in those cultures were responsible for putting food on the table, and so the gods in those cultures were generally understood to be female. But then the plow was invented, which was pulled by an animal. When women used this new invention, it required significantly more physical effort, and as a result miscarriage rates increased. So men took over working the plow, which led to the gods being perceived as male.

These forms and expressions come and go over time
because our conceptions of God and the images we
use to picture and explain those conceptions are deeply
shaped by the patterns, technologies, and customs of the
world we live in.

And so there are masculine images of God—Jesus prayed
to his "Father in heaven"—
and there are feminine images of God—
the prophet Isaiah quotes God saying,
"Can a mother forget the baby at her breast
and have no compassion on the child she has borne?
Though she may forget,
I will not forget you!"

When God is described as
father or
mother or
judge or
potter or
rock or
fortress or
warrior or
refuge or
strength or
friend or
lawgiver,
those writers are taking something they've seen,
something they've experienced, and they're essentially
saying, "God is like *that*."

It's an attempt to put that which is beyond language into a frame or form we can grasp.

An image of God doesn't contain God,
in the same way a word about God or a doctrine or a dogma about God isn't God; it only points to God.

Whatever we say about God always rests within the larger reality of what we can't say;
meaning always resides within a larger mystery;
knowing always takes place within unknowing;
whatever has been revealed to us surrounded by that which hasn't been revealed to us.

When you hear about a teenage girl being kidnapped and sold into the sex trade, it makes you really, really angry, correct? It breaks your heart, right? And you know it: you *know* that it's wrong, evil, corrupt, vile, and violating to all of us in some way.

You're *sure* of it.

I know a man named Charlie who is in his late fifties. When he was fifty-five, he and his wife Kim became deeply grieved by how many orphans there are in the world. And so they started adopting kids from all over the globe. They currently have five children and they're in the process of adopting two more. When you see their family coming, it's like a mini United Nations. There is something tangibly divine about what they're doing.

We do know things—
we know them with every fiber in our being—
they're revealed to us,
they seize us and they won't let us go.
They haunt us,
they capture us,
they plant themselves deep in our hearts and
they don't leave.

So when we talk about God,
we're talking about our brushes with spirit,
our awareness of the reverence humming within us,
our sense of the nearness
and the farness,
that which we know
and that which is unknown,
that which we can talk about
and that which eludes the grasp of our words,
that which is crystal-clear
and that which is more mysterious than ever.

And sometimes language helps,
and sometimes language fails.

————

Several points, then, about *how* we talk about God.

First, it's important for us to acknowledge that when we
talk about God, we often find ourselves in the middle of
one paradox after another.

Near and far,
known and unknown,
words and silence,
answers and questions,
that which is deeply mysterious and ambiguous
and that which is right in front of us as plain as day.

I point this out because the dominant consciousness of
our world continues to perceive and process reality in
mostly either/or categories—we want to know whose side
you are on, which one is *the* answer, how the tension is
going to be resolved, how the paradox will be eliminated.

But some truths don't fit in a twenty-second sound bite
on television.

Take faith, for example. For many people in our world,
the opposite of faith is doubt. The goal, then, within this
understanding, is to eliminate doubt. But faith and doubt
aren't opposites. Doubt is often a sign that your faith
has a pulse, that it's alive and well and exploring and
searching. Faith and doubt aren't opposites; they are, it
turns out, excellent dance partners.

Back to paradox, and an observation about our world
today: fundamentalism shouldn't surprise us. When a
leader comes along who eliminates the tension and
dodges the paradox and neatly and precisely explains
who the enemies are and gives black-and-white answers
to questions, leaving little room for the very real mystery

of the divine, it should not surprise us when that person gains a large audience.

Especially if that person is really, really confident.

Certainty is easier, faster, awesome for fundraising, and it often generates large amounts of energy because who doesn't want to be right?

Which leads us back to our original insight that *how* you believe and *what* you believe are two different things. Two people can believe the same thing but hold that belief in very different ways.

You can believe something with so much conviction that you'd die for that belief,

and yet in the exact same moment

you can also say, "I could be wrong . . ."

This is because conviction and humility, like faith and doubt, are not opposites; they're dance partners. It's possible to hold your faith with open hands, living with great conviction and yet at the same time humbly admitting that your knowledge and perspective will always be limited.

Do you believe the exact same things you did in the exact same way you did five years ago?

Probably not.

You've grown,
evolved,
changed,
had new experiences,
studied,
listened,
observed,
suffered,
reflected,
and reexamined.

That's how faith is.
We learn as we go.

Years ago I was struggling—really, really struggling to make sense of a number of things in my life, in a lot of pain. I started going to a counselor who gradually helped me understand why I was feeling how I was feeling and how I got there and what a better future might look like. It was, as I look back on that period now, truly life-changing. My counselor, who has become like family to me, wasn't ever pushy or judgmental or condemning, and he never tried to get me to believe exactly as he does. And yet he had no problem looking me in the eyes and challenging me and confronting me and pointing out when I was way, way off base. He was kind and humble and open, and yet firm and rock solid and unshakable.

All at the same time.

He was a man of faith,
deeply grounded in his convictions,
and yet those firm convictions didn't close him down or
harden him or make him brittle and closed-minded; they
had the exact opposite effect. They seemed to make him
more flexible and limber and engaging.

Like a tree,
planted near water,
with deep roots.
A storm comes and the tree doesn't break because it's
grounded enough to . . . bend.

I believe that this is one of the most urgent questions
people are asking at this time about the very nature of
faith: Can conviction and humility coexist as the dance
partners we need them to be?

I say yes, they can. I have seen it up close, and it's
possible. It requires that we pay as much attention to
how we are talking as to *what* we are talking about, and
it requires us to leave the paradox as it is, the tension
unresolved, holding our convictions with humility.

All of which leads me to something my friend Pete wrote:

When it comes to talking about God, that which we cannot speak of is the one thing about whom and to whom we must never stop talking.

So now, with that said,

and not said,

on to the God who is **with** us.

CHAPTER 4

WITH

So finally, after
Open
and
Both,
we get to
With
and
For
and
Ahead.

I remember years ago hearing someone tell a dramatic story about something incredible that had happened in his life, and the way he summarized what had happened was "... and then God showed up!" It was moving to hear how thrilled he was, but I had one of those "Wait—what?" moments soon afterward. If God *showed up,* then prior to that, was God somewhere else? And if God was somewhere else, and then God came here for that person at that moment, why didn't God show up for all of those other people in all of those other moments who could have used some showing up?

I've encountered this conception of God countless times over the years, a perspective that isn't as much about *who* God is as *where* God is. I've heard people pray and ask God to *be with them;* I've heard songs inviting God to *come near;* I've heard a good event described as a *God thing*—all of these undergirded by the subtle yet powerful belief that God is somewhere else and then comes here to this world from time to time to do God sorts of things.

The problem with this as one's *only* conception of God is that it raises endless questions about when and where and why God chooses to act.

Or not act.

I don't know why the Holocaust happened or why that young girl was abducted or why that uncle got a brain tumor. And neither do you. None of us does. And anybody who can tell you why God decided to come here and act in one instance but not another should not be trusted. Lots of people were given *only this particular conception* of God at some point in their lives and they're still living with it: that God is somewhere else and may or may not come here from time to time to do God sorts of things.

Do you see what this leads to?

This conception of God can easily lead people to the notion that life, the world, existence, etc. is perfectly capable of going on without *that* God. *That* God becomes, in essence, *optional*.

That God may or may not exist.

Great effort, then, is often spent trying to prove that *that* God even exists, which can, of course, fail spectacularly.

————————

There is, I believe, another way to see God, a way in which we see God with us—**with** us, right here, right now. This isn't just an idea to me; this is an urgent, passionate, ecstatic invitation to wake up, to see the world as it truly is.

I recently bought some new snorkeling gear, and as I was pulling it out of its packaging a little tube of something fell out. I was so excited to get to the water that I didn't think anything of that fallen tube as I grabbed the gear and headed out. I got to the beach, put on the fins, adjusted the mask, and made sure the snorkel was firmly attached, and then I dove in, expecting to see the reef below in stunning color and detail.

But I couldn't.

I could make out shapes and a bit of color, but otherwise my mask wouldn't stop fogging up. It was then, out in the water, several hundred feet from shore, that I remembered that little tube, which I realized was a special solvent I'd heard about—one you wipe on the mask so that it won't fog.

Having interacted with literally thousands of people over the years as a pastor, I've often felt like my job was to help people discover where they dropped that little tube, because seeing is the first step to pretty much everything.

I want *you* to see.

Not in a superficial, check-the-box, oh-yeah-now-I-get-it casual sort of way, but in an "Oh dear God, my eyes are finally open" sort of way.

To explore this seeing and what it means for each of us, let's first go to the dining room table at my friend Rosa's house. Rosa is Italian and she's an amazing cook—that's a bit redundant, isn't it?—and she makes these huge meals that take hours to eat while her husband John goes back and forth from the kitchen bringing plate after plate of food and inevitably—usually sometime around the first round of dessert—someone will mention how *transcendent* or *out of this world* or *sublime* or *divine* or *glorious* the meal has been.

I imagine you've had similar experiences that you would use similar words to describe—maybe you were holding a newborn child or hearing a favorite song performed live or standing on the side of a mountain or floating in a lake or even washing dishes on an average day when you became aware of something else going on, something more, something just below the surface of whatever it was you were experiencing—something you'd say was sublime or glorious or transcendent.

Sometimes it's extreme, adrenaline-inducing moments, like the other day when I was out on the ocean paddling on my board and I heard a sound I'd never heard before. Like a wheezy two-pack-a-day uncle clearing his throat, only louder and *lower*. More subterranean rumble than cough. As I turned around to see water shooting up from the surface, I realized that I was close—really, really close—to a whale.

So I did what anybody would do in that situation: I paddled closer. (Which my wife Kristen would probably point out is *not* what most people would do.) My heart was beating furiously like the kick drum in one of those early Metallica songs. As I glided along next to the whale, I was overwhelmed by a sense of what I would call *acute smallness*. The dark bluish-blackish color of its skin, the sheer volume of water it displaced when it came to the surface, and the size of my board in comparison to its size all conspired to impress upon me:

"You, Rob, are a very, very small being in a very, very large world."

Other times it isn't the adrenaline-producing mountaintop and whale moments; it's the times we're overwhelmed by depth and intensity of feeling at the other end of the spectrum. I recently went to lunch with a friend at one of my favorite taco places. About twenty minutes into lunch, he began to tell me about the unraveling of his marriage. He told me about their history together and how it got them to this point and what it's doing to her and what it's doing to him and what it's like for him to go grocery shopping and then go back to his new apartment, all alone.

Somewhere in our conversation the full force of what he was saying hit me—divorce, the effect on their kids, the image of both of them at some point *taking off* their wedding rings. It was as if our interaction up until that point had taken place in my mind, but all of a sudden it dropped with a dull thud down into my heart and I was engulfed by sheer, unadulterated sadness and sorrow that permeated my entire being.

I choked up, right there in my favorite taco place.

There are the highs,
there are the lows,
and then there are the normal, average, everyday
moments like washing dishes or making your kids

breakfast or walking the dog or giving the neighbor kid a high five when you find yourself catching glimpses, clues, and glances of depth and dimension and fullness.

Sometimes it catches you off guard; sometimes it sneaks up on you from behind; sometimes you find yourself slowing down and becoming gripped with a certain stillness, like your heart is slamming on the brakes while it whispers in your ear, "This matters, this is significant, slow down, pay attention," like your soul is trying to take a picture because of the realization that *whatever's going on here right now is worth capturing.*

When we try to describe these moments and we use words like *transcendent* and we talk about something being *out of this world* or about an event as having *depth* or being *sublime,* what we're talking about is our sense that
it is what it is,
but it is also,
at the same time,
something more.

It was a meal, but it was more than a meal,
in the same way that it was just a conversation,
and yet it was more than just a conversation.

You were there, fully present, taking in every tactile dimension of the experience, and yet your visceral, physical experience drew you higher, farther, beyond that very same experience.

It's as if the present, real-time, flesh-and-blood taste of that meal around Rosa's table somehow pointed *past* itself, its vitality and joy an echo of a larger vitality and joy.

In November of 2011, I was walking through the second floor of the Phoenix Art Museum when I came across a massive wall of pink and yellow that appeared to be changing color. As I walked toward it, I began to see that the wall was actually an installation, about fifteen feet tall by thirty feet wide, made entirely of sheets of paper—thousands of them, maybe millions of them, some yellow and some pink, all stacked and arranged with great care and precision to produce this particular effect. It was mesmerizing. So simple and yet so genius. Who does that? Who decides to stack that many sheets in such a precise, intentional order? Who has that kind of patience? And how did the artist know it would produce such an emotional reaction?

It was just a wall of stacked sheets of paper,
and yet it was more than just a wall of stacked sheets of paper,
in the same way that it's just a song,
and yet it's more than just a collection of notes, noises, and melodies.

To be as precise as possible, then, I imagine you're like me in that you regularly find yourself having experiences that **point past themselves to a larger reference point, to something or somewhere or sometime or someone beyond the experience itself in its most basic essence.**

These moments have a familiar paradox inherent within them, in that they are both
near and far,
close and distant,
right here and yet somewhere else,
all at the same time.

(Have you noticed how often first-time parents speak of being over the moon? What does a tiny infant have to do with outer space?)

Often you can touch these experiences,
hold them,
lean on them,
sing along with them,
breathe them in,
see them in their proximity and nearness,
and yet they have a compelling way of leading you beyond them, as if they were a window or a door into another room.

———————

The ancient Hebrews, it turns out, had a way of talking about these experiences we've all had, those moments when we become aware that there's more going on here, moments when an object or gesture or word or event is what it is and yet points beyond itself.

They believed that everything you and I know to be everything that is exists because of an explosive, expansive, surprising, creative energy that surges through all things, holding everything all together and giving the universe its life and depth and fullness.

They called this cosmic electricity,
this expressed power,
this divine energy,
the **ruach** of God.

They believed that this divine *ruach* flows from God because, as the writer says in the Psalms, the whole earth is God's, all of it infused with *ruach,* crammed with restless creative energy, full of unquenchable life force and unending divine vitality, undergirded and electrified by the God who continually renews the face of the earth.

When the Hebrews talked about the world, then, they didn't talk about a world that went on day after day doing its thing while they discussed whether or not there was a God out there somewhere who might or might not exist. What they talked about was all of this life and vitality and creativity and stars and rocks and talking and pasta and tears and whales having a singular, common, creative, sustaining source—whom they called God—who powers and energizes and sustains it all.

And that *all* includes us.

While they understood this *ruach* energy to be as wide as the universe and powerful enough to fuel and animate and sustain even the stars, as it's written in the Psalms, they also understood this *ruach* to be as intimate and personal as the breath you just took and the breath you're about to take.

In fact, they often referred to *ruach* as breath, as in the story of Job, where it's written,

> As long as I have life within me,
> the *ruach* of God in my nostrils . . .

The wisdom teacher in Ecclesiastes echoed this understanding in writing that every single one of us is the recipient of this energy and life force and divine breath, given to us by God to sustain us and fill us and enrich us and inspire us and give us life.

We all, the Hebrews insisted—before we do or say or create or accomplish anything—have been given a gift, as close as our breath, as real as life itself.

But breath wasn't the only way they understood *ruach*. In many cases they used the word to refer to what we would call *spirit,* although that word *spirit* can bring with it a number of associations in our world that the Hebrews didn't have. In our modern world, many people understand *spirit* to mean something less real, less tangible, less substantive—something nonphysical, often relegated to the realm of religion. Something that may or may not exist.

But *ruach* doesn't divide the world up like that.
In Job God's *ruach* garnishes the heavens,
and in the Psalms it's the *ruach* that brings things into existence.

When they spoke of the *ruach* of God, they weren't talking about something less real; they were talking about what happens when something becomes more real right before your eyes.

When they spoke of *ruach,* they weren't talking about an abstract realm somewhere else; they were talking about the giant megaphone parked one millimeter from your ear, announcing to you in clearly pronounced, unmistakable sounds that *this is real* and it is happening and it is not to be denied or dismissed.

When they spoke of *ruach,* as the poet does in the first lines of the Bible, they were talking about the very life force that brings everything into existence, the presence of God within the world, dwelling in every created being, present to everyone and everything all the time.

They repeatedly spoke of this presence of God
everywhere in all places, events, and beings. As one of
the Psalm writers asked,

> Where can I go from your spirit,
> where can I flee from your presence?
> If I go up to the heavens,
> you are there;
> if I make my bed in the depths,
> you are there . . .

(It's important to note that the Hebrews were careful not
to say that God *is* the flower or sunset or pasta or lump in
the throat—they didn't say God *is* creation, because they
understood that in giving life to everything, God also
gives creation freedom to be whatever it's going to be,
with all of the possibilities and potentials for good and
bad and beauty and chaos and love and loss that that
freedom might lead to.)

All of which leads me back to the start, to where we
began, to the simple, straightforward belief that God is
with us.

I believe God is with us,
around us,
beside us,
present with us in every moment.

The question, then,
the art,
the task,
the search,
the challenge,
the invitation is for you and me to become more and more the kind of people who are *aware* of the divine presence, attuned to the *ruach,* present to the depths of each and every moment, seeing God in more and more and more people, places, and events, each and every day.

Several thoughts about this seeing.

First, **what our experiences of God do at the most primal level of consciousness is jolt us into the affirmation that whatever *this* is, it matters.** This person, place, event, gesture, attitude, action, piece of art, parcel of land, heart, word, moment—it matters.

When my wife Kristen was fifteen, she went on her first date with a guy she knew from school. He came to her house, picked her up, they went to a movie, and then he drove her homeward. Her family lived in the desert at the time, and on the way home, on a remote stretch of road several miles from her house, a drunk driver coming the other way crossed the centerline and hit them head-on. The cars were totaled and Kristen and her date were rushed in an ambulance to the hospital. Her parents, who were called by the first responders, quickly got in their car and headed for the hospital, down the very same road Kristen and her date had just been driving on. Several miles from their house Kristen's parents saw a commotion up ahead in the road—commotion that they soon realized was due to the car their daughter had been riding in, which hadn't yet been removed from the road. And so they passed by the smashed relic of a car their daughter had been in moments earlier when she was hit head-on by a drunk driver going way over fifty miles an hour.

My mother-in-law Judie told me that it's the first time she'd ever seen Kristen's dad with a tear in his eye.

I tell you this story because Kristen's father has always loved his daughter, and at any point in her life if you'd asked him if she mattered to him he would have said, "Yes, of course." I imagine as well that if you'd ever asked him if she could matter any more to him, he would have said, "No, I can't imagine how." And yet we can safely assume that in that moment, as he drove by the wreckage of that car with a tear in his eye, his daughter somehow mattered *more* to him than before.

It's like there's a scale from 1 to 10, and you always would have sworn that someone or something mattered to you with a 10. But then you almost (or you actually do) lose her or him or it or them, and suddenly your heart is filled with a 17 or a 39 or a 4,291 kind of mattering. New capacities, ones you didn't know were possible before, open up inside of you.

Sometimes you realize that something that *didn't* seem to matter to you actually *does* matter, other times something that mattered to you suddenly finds a way to matter even *more* to you, but every time something within you *expands.*

The ancient Hebrews had a word for this awareness of the importance of things. They called it *kavod. Kavod* originally was a business term, referring to the heaviness of something, which was crucial in weights and measures and the maintaining of fairness in transactions. Over time the word began to take on a more figurative meaning, referring to the importance and significance of something.

Kavod is what happens when you're exchanging the usual "How are yous?" with a person you see regularly, only on this particular day she doesn't respond with her normal "Fine, and you?" but instead says, "Not good"—and suddenly everything changes. Now you ask her why she *isn't* good and she tells you and you quickly find yourself in the midst of her pain and you feel what she's feeling and you hurt like she hurts and the conversation is no longer brief and shallow like it has been for years, because now it *weighs* something, it is significant, it matters.

She matters;
you matter;
the fact that she decided to be honest with you matters;
the thing that is happening between you matters.

That's *kavod.*

Kavod is what happens when you're trying to talk someone out of suicide and you keep insisting that his life matters. You're trying to find better ways to explain it and you're begging and pleading and persuading and doing your best to convince him not to go through with it—and you keep coming back to the conviction you have that life matters, even though that sounds so simple and *duh* and obvious in the moment.

It's what happens when you meet up with someone who has just shaved his head and you make a joke about it and he tells you that it's because a friend of his is going through chemo and his shaved head is a sign of solidarity—and suddenly you're staring at that shiny head in a whole new way.

That's *kavod.*

We live in a *lite* world—one that bombards us from thousands of directions with advertisements and escape in every conceivable form and television shows about people doing mindless things and elevators that play mind-numbing versions of songs we used to like before we heard them a million times. This noise, in all its visual and psychic forms, can numb us, making this day feel like it's *without weight* because it's just like all the others as they all run together.

But *kavod, kavod* is something else.

Kavod is serious—not in an overbearing, stilted kind of way but in a sacred, holy kind of way. The word is often used in the scriptures to refer to God's *glory*—that which happens when the monotony is pierced, the boredom hijacked, the despair overpowered by your sense that something else is going on, just below the surface, something that's bigger and wider and deeper and more powerful than anything you could begin to imagine. Something that reminds you of your smallness, frailty, and impermanence. It's that gut-level awareness you're seized by that tells you, "Pay attention, because this matters."

When we're talking about God, we're talking about every single one of those moments—whether they're earth-shatteringly loud and large or infinitesimally small and whisper-like, mere slivers you inadvertently stumble upon—
moments when you are convinced, even if you've been burned and
let down and
betrayed countless times—
that cynicism does not have the last word, that life is not random or meaningless or empty, but that what you do and how you feel and what you say and where you go and what you make of this life you've been given *matters*.

This realization—that things matter—leads us to a **second particular response** our brushes with *ruach* provoke within us, one that takes me to a small city in Virginia I recently visited for the first time.

As I drove up to the town square, I noticed that it was crowded with tents full of people who were camping out to protest the growing economic inequality in our country. Later that evening, a number of the protesters came marching through the center of town, shouting and chanting and singing about injustice and poverty and greed and the ways that those things tear at the fabric of our common life together.

Shortly after that I was talking with a friend who had just recently joined a food co-op where participants pay a monthly fee and then receive delivery of a wide variety of fruits and vegetables and grains from local farms. She was raving about the quality and freshness of the food and how much less the food had to travel because it was locally sourced and how that cut down on the carbon footprint and how that was teaching her about the farming community that was just a few miles from where she lived.

And then shortly after that, I ran into a young couple who were toting around their newborn son and I did what we all do—I made the obligatory comments about how cute he was and how much he resembled his mom and dad, and then I inevitably grabbed his little hand and held it up and said, "It's so small!" as if I were surprised.

Why do I always do that? Was I expecting his hand to be large? I bet you do the same thing.

You hold up that hand and you stare at it and you talk about how small it is and what a marvel it is and how you can't get over the miracle of new life, etc., etc. Why do we do this?

We do this because it's not just about the baby.

We hold up the baby's hand and marvel at it because it reconnects us with the wondrous mystery that is our own life.

**New life is deeply moving and mysterious because
all life is deeply moving and mysterious.**

We hold that newborn baby's hand up for the same reason that protesters march and people join food co-ops—because **we have an intuitive awareness that everything is ultimately connected to everything else, and I believe that is one more clue to who it is we're talking about when we talk about God.**

How we eat is connected to how we care for the planet which is connected to how we use our resources

which is connected to how many people in the world go to bed hungry every night
which is connected to how food is distributed
which is connected to the massive inequalities in our world between those who have and those who don't
which is connected to how our justice system treats people who use their power and position to make hundreds of millions of dollars while others struggle just to buy groceries
which is connected to how we treat those who don't have what we have
which is connected to the sanctity and holiness and mystery of our human life and their human life and his little human life
which is why we hold up that baby's hand and say to the parents, "It's just so small."

There's an ancient Jewish prayer that begins,

> Hear, O Israel:
> the Zad D our God,
> the Lad D is *one*.

One is the English translation for the Hebrew word *echad,* which refers to a unity made up of many parts. The oneness the Shema prayer refers to is important because it makes a clear distinction between God and everything else that exists—preserving the beauty and transcendence and otherness of God while at the same time speaking to our sense that all of the diversity and difference and pulsating creativity we know to be life comes from a common, singular source and center who is one in a way that nothing else is one.

This is one of the reasons we watch movies, attend recovery groups, read memoirs, and sit around campfires telling stories long after the fire has dwindled down to a few glowing embers. It's written in the Psalms that "deep calls to deep," which is what happens when you get a glimpse of what someone else has gone through or is currently in the throes of and you find yourself inextricably, mysteriously linked with that person because you have been reminded again of our common humanity and its singular source, the subsurface unity of all things that is ever before us in countless manifestations but requires eyes wide open to see it burst into view.

We live in a dis-integrated culture, in which headlines and opinions and images and sound bites pound us with their fragmented, frantic, isolated blips and squeaks, none of it bound together by any higher unity, coherence, or transcendent reference point.

This fragmentation can easily shape us, convincing us that things aren't one.

But when we talk about God, we're talking about the very straightforward affirmation that everything has a singular, common source and is infinitely, endlessly, deeply connected.

We are involved, all of us.
And it all matters,
and it's all connected.

All of which leads me to a **third particular response**
to *ruach,* one that takes me to Long Beach, California,
to a TED conference. Each February over a thousand
people gather at this conference to listen to some of
the brightest, most creative, most innovative people
in the world give talks on technology, environment,
design, science, and a number of other topics. It's an
extraordinary thing to sit for a week and hear scientists
and inventors and writers sharing what they've
discovered and created and pioneered and achieved in
their efforts to make the world a better place.

There's also an agreement, I'm assuming unspoken, that
God and religion aren't to be acknowledged beyond
passing, often apologetic references to spirituality and
transcendence. These are, after all, the smartest folks
around. What would Jesus have to do with anything
they're doing? (That is an example of sarcasm.)

I tell you all this because at TED 2012 a brilliant,
passionate lawyer named Bryan Stevenson gave a talk
about injustice and racism. He spoke about his work
around the country within the prison and court systems
and his desire to see all people treated fairly. He told
stories about young men he's currently defending in
court, arguing compellingly for a more just society, and

then he closed with a quote from Martin Luther King Jr. (who was quoting the abolitionist Theodore Parker) about how the moral arc of the universe is long and it bends toward justice.

The second Stevenson was done, the audience gave him a rousing, extended standing ovation. Then later, they pitched in collectively to give his organization over a million dollars.

I point this out because when the audience was asked from the stage two days earlier how many of them considered themselves religious, it appeared that only about 2 or 3 percent of the people raised their hands.

And yet a man confronted them with the *moral arc of the universe* and they intuitively, unanimously, instantly affirmed the truth of his claim.

Is history headed somewhere?
Seriously?

Because when Bryan Stevenson talks about the moral arc of the universe, he's talking about history, history that is headed somewhere, somewhere good.

History that has a point to it.

I believe that those smart, educated, accomplished, self-described-as-not-very-religious people stood and applauded because deep within every single one of us is the conviction that there is a point to this. That life has purpose. That when we die, the lights are not turned off and the show is not over.

The Greeks had a word for this sense of forward movement, purpose, and direction—they called it *telos*. The *telos* of something is its point, its purpose, where it's headed, what it's doing, and where it's going.

This is why we love stories: they're loaded with *telos.* They are not static but dynamic realities, heavy with potential and possibility. In a story, something happens, and then something else happens after that, leading somewhere. That's how stories work.

When we talk about God, we're talking about that sense you have—however stifled, faint, or repressed it is—that hope is real, that things are headed somewhere, and that that somewhere is good.

That's the power of a TV show like *The Office.* Boring meetings and photocopiers that hum in the background and annoying people in the next cubicle—at the deepest level these sorts of settings are a vise on our heart, squeezing us tighter and tighter with the insistence that tomorrow is going to be just like today. It's the terror of the modern world, the crushing fear behind every day: that it's going to be like this—just like this—tomorrow and the next day and the next day.

And so a show about a drab and dreary office where the work is mind-numbing and the rewards meaningless— and yet the people stuck in this setting find humanity and laughter and compassion and even meaning—has a really, really powerful effect on its viewers.

When light bursts through,
when our boredom is pierced and our angst hijacked by surprise,
we're brushing up against *ruach*—
calling us,
inviting us,
rescuing us,
reminding us
that

it all matters,
it's all connected,
and it's all headed somewhere.

———

To wrap up this chapter about the God who is with us, then, a few thoughts.

First, I began this chapter by talking about our very real experiences of this world for a very specific reason: **I believe that you are *already experiencing* the presence of God with you in countless ways every single day.** This is why I introduced you to *ruach* and the idea that God is the source of the very *going-on-*

ness of the universe, like electricity that powers the whole house and everything in it.

There's a story about Jesus where he's at a dinner party, reclining at the table with the other guests, when a woman begins pouring perfume on his head. His disciples are outraged because of how expensive the perfume is. Jesus, however, is thrilled, telling them, "She has done a beautiful thing to me." He then proceeds to tell them that what she's done is prepare him for burial.

Burial? Here's the revealing part: in Jesus's day, preparing someone for burial was a *religious* act. In Jesus's eyes, this woman's gesture is a holy, sacred act of worship. His disciples miss this, seeing only a common, everyday act.

They miss the power and significance of the moment because
they don't have the eyes to see what's going on right in front of them.

There is a strong word here in this story for our day: you can be very religious and invoke the name of God and be able to quote lots of verses and be well versed in complicated theological systems and yet not be a person who *sees*.
It's one thing to sing about God and recite quotes about God and invoke God's name; it's another to be aware of the presence in every taste, touch, sound, and embrace.

With Jesus, what we see again and again is that it's never
just a person, or
just a meal, or
just an event,
because **there's always more going on just below the
surface.**

Jesus sees what others miss.
He is aware when others are oblivious.

I love how the apostle Paul puts it in a letter to friends:
"May the eyes of your heart be enlightened."

Which leads me to a second point, one about faith.
Sometimes people who believe in God are referred to as
"people of faith." Which isn't the whole truth, because
everybody **has faith.**

To believe in God requires faith. To experience this world
and its endless surprise and mystery and depth and then
emphatically declare that is has *no* common source,
it is *not* headed somewhere, and it ultimately has *no*
meaning—that takes faith as well.

I tell you this because in the times I found myself in the
deepest, darkest places of doubt and despair, it seemed
too huge a leap of faith to trust that there is a God who
loves and helps and hears and heals. That sounded crazy
to me. Depending on where you're coming from, that

kind of faith can seem naive, simple, childish, uninformed, and at times downright stupid.

In those times, believing in God to me seemed like taking a flying leap.

But the truth is, I had already taken a leap, because we've *all* taken a leap. Whatever it is that we believe, whatever it is that we trust, we've all leaped and we're endlessly leaping because we are all people of faith.

Whether you believe that this is all there is
or
we come from outer space
or
you're a Christian or a Buddhist or you're Jewish or Jedi
or
you don't believe that we can know *anything* for sure,
it's all a form of faith.

Nobody *hasn't* leaped.

Which leads me to one more thought about the God who's with us: choosing to trust that this life matters and we're all connected and this is all headed somewhere has made my life way, way better.

Or to say it another way, God has made my life better.

I don't mean this in a shallow, trite, then-I-believed-and-now-I'm-happy-all-the-time way, but in a deep, abiding, satisfying way.

I move more slowly than I used to because I don't want to miss anything.
I find more and more beauty and meaning in everyday, average moments that I would have missed before.
I need fewer answers because I see more.
I find more people more fascinating than ever because I'm more and more used to being surprised by the mystery that a human being is.
I've discovered more and more events are less about the events themselves and more about me being open to whatever it is that's going on just below the surface.

Because there's always something more,
something else,
depth and fullness and life,
right there,
all of it a gift from the God who is **with** us.

CHAPTER 5

FOR

Now, on to the God who I believe is **for** us.

When you've heard people talk about God, did they talk
clearly and compellingly about the God who is for us?
The God who is for all of humanity and wants the best
for everybody—regardless of their background or religion
or perspective or beliefs or what they've done or haven't
done?

Do you believe that God is for *you*?
Do you believe that God's desire is that you flourish,
thrive, shine?
Do you believe that God wants you to be everything you
could possibly be as you become more and more and
more your true self?

I do.

While this is very simple and straightforward, for a staggering number of people in our world the *for* of the Jesus message has been buried under a massive pile of *against*s. Somewhere in all of the years of religious againstness—from boycotts and wars and judgments and sermons about how "God loves you if you'll just . . ." and "God is for you as long as you . . ." and inquisitions and placards and crusades and terrible PR—for many people the beautiful, life-changing message of God being *for* us has been lost.

All of which means it's time for a radical reclaiming of the fundamental Christian message that God is for us.

God, according to Jesus, is for us because God loves us.

Once again, this is rather straightforward and simple, and yet ask average people on the street what the first thing is that comes to mind when they hear the word *Christian,* and it's tragic how few will mention something about the revolutionary news at the heart of Jesus's message: that God is for us.

I realize that in asking that question and talking about God being for us, it's easy to sound like a motivational speaker or a salesperson or a televangelist—promising all of these AMAZING! THINGS! that are going to happen to YOU! if you just believe . . .
or have enough faith . . .

or give money . . .
or blindly follow . . .
or pray or whatever.

So let me first say that when I talk about God being *for*
us, I'm not talking about guarantees and surefire ways
to stay healthy and have lots of friends and drive a nice
car and keep up with the Kardashians. When I talk about
flourishing and thriving and shining, I'm talking about
something much more profound, enduring, meaningful,
and satisfying.

And to talk about that—
about God being *for* us—
I'll talk about the God that Jesus talked about,
which means I'll first talk about Jesus,
which means I need to tell you about something that
happens in the town I live in on the first Friday night in
the month of December.

———

On that first Friday night the businesses and shops and
restaurants throw a party. They close down the streets
in the center of town and Santa rides in (as he does in all
those Bible verses), and the stores serve food and drinks
and play Christmas music.

Last year, one of the surf shops topped them all by
bringing in a gospel choir to sing among the racks of

T-shirts and trunks. The store was packed. And the choir was amazing. At one point, they sang a Christmas hymn in which Jesus is referred to as *Immanuel,* which is an ancient Hebrew word that means *God with us.*

Picture your average nativity scene, assembled sometime in late November or early December, sitting in someone's front yard or on the lawn of a church, with a spotlight or two shining on it. There are a few animals, some wise men (three, for some reason), Mary—who has just traveled miles on dusty roads but is wearing a spotless white-and-blue robe, Joseph—who apparently found time during the birth to trim his beard, and then there, in the middle of it all, lying in a manger, is

—in the words of the great poet Ricky Bobby—

> Eight-pound six-ounce newborn infant . . .
> don't even know a word yet . . .
> golden fleece diapers with your tiny fat balled-up fist

baby Jesus,

whose birth is celebrated every year at Christmas in a variety of ways, some of them even having something to do with Jesus.

This ritual is so familiar,
so predictable,
so harmless,

so *benign,*
that it's easy to miss how this word *Immanuel* is actually
an extremely radical claim about the very nature of
reality.

Right there in that surf shop, jammed to the walls with
people smiling and nodding along, those singers in their
Christmas song were singing about
the divine
and the human
existing in the same place.

In the same *body.*

This Christmas story, then, the one that we're all so
familiar with, is a deeply subversive account, coming in
just under the radar, giving us a picture of a God who
is not distant or detached or indifferent to our pain or
uninterested in our condition or uninvolved in our very
real struggles in this world, but instead is present among
us in Jesus to
teach us
and help us
and suffer with us
and give us hope
because
this God is *for* us.

So when we talk about Jesus being divine and human,
what we're saying is that Jesus, in a

unique,
singular, and
historic way,
shows us what God is like.

And to talk about what God is like,
let's talk about waterskiing.

———————

If you've water-skied before, I assume you remember
your first time, floating there in the water, teeth
chattering, life jacket strangling you up to your jawbone,
being told to keep the rope between your skis. And
what was the advice that the people in the boat kept
repeating? Remember? (Say it with me now . . .)

"Let the boat pull you up!"

Which the people in the boat, who have done this before,
say like it's the most sensible thing imaginable, but which,
to someone who has never water-skied, can sound like
complete nonsense.

Lean back—to go forward?
Stay down—to get up?

As a result of this confusion, many people, on their first
attempt, get pulled forward out over the front of their
skis; they ignore the advice from the boat and follow

their natural inclination, which is to try to get themselves up onto the surface of the water.

Which doesn't work, because you *can't* get yourself on your own up onto the surface of the water.

It's impossible.

Learning to water-ski requires a person to make the counterintuitive leap from trying to do what seems natural, which is to get yourself up onto the surface of the water, to trusting that the boat will do that work for you.

Which can take a few tries and often involves a lot of water up your suit.

I talk about the counterintuitive nature of learning to water-ski because at the heart of what Jesus teaches us about God is something called *gospel*. Gospel is an unexpected, foreign notion, a strange idea that cuts against many of the dominant ways we've all come to believe are how the world works.

In one of his first teachings, Jesus announces God's blessing on those he calls the "poor in spirit." The poor in spirit are those who are lacking, who don't have it all together, who are acutely aware of how they don't measure up.
The nobodies,

the pathetic,
the lame,
the has-beens,
the not-good-enoughs.

This word *blessing* he uses is a rich, evocative, loaded word, and it essentially means "God is on your side."

I talk about gospel—Jesus's announcement of good news and blessing for everybody who needs it—because over the years as a pastor I've interacted with thousands of people who were operating under the conviction that if they could just get *better*—
more moral,
more disciplined,
more spiritual,
more kind,
more courageous,
more holy or righteous or whatever religious jargon they had picked up along the way—
then they would be
in
or
accepted
or
embraced
or
validated
or

affirmed
by God.

I've often been asked, "Isn't the only thing that really matters to God in the end that you're a good person?"

This sounds great, and being and doing good are obviously central to what it means to be human, but can you hear the other thing, the subtle belief system, just below the surface of this sensible, common, conventional way of seeing God?

That question often flows from a belief that God operates according to a point or merit system, and if you do the good or right or decent or religious thing, then you will get the points you need to get on God's good side.

That is not gospel.

Gospel is the shocking, provocative, revolutionary, subversive, counterintuitive good news that in your moments of greatest
despair,
failure,
sin,
weakness,
losing,
failing,
frustration,

inability,
helplessness,
wandering,
and falling short,
God meets you *there*—
right there—
right exactly there—
in *that* place, and announces,
I am on your side.

Gospel insists that God doesn't wait for us to get ourselves polished, shined, proper, and without blemish— God comes to us and meets us and blesses us while we are still in the middle of the mess we created.

Gospel isn't us getting it together so that we can have God's favor; gospel is us finding God exactly in the moment of our greatest *not-togetherness*.

Gospel is grace, and grace is a gift. You don't earn a gift; you simply receive it. You don't make it happen; you wake up to what has already happened.

Gospel isn't doing enough good to be worthy; it's your eyes being opened to your unworthiness and to Jesus's insistence that that was never the way it worked in the first place.

Being a good person, then, naturally flows not from trying to get on God's good side but from your realization that God has been on your side the whole time.

Gospel calls you to a major change in thinking,
a giant shift in understanding,
a massive leap in how you see yourself—
otherwise, you're stuck in the same old points program, trying to earn what is already yours.

Can you see why Jesus often began his teachings by saying "Repent!"? You know what *repent* means? It means to change your thinking, to see things in a new way, to have your mind renewed—all of which reminds me of my first Alcoholics Anonymous meeting.

———————

I was twenty-five years old, just starting out as a pastor, and one evening after I'd given a sermon, a man named George walked up to me and told me that I needed to go to an AA meeting. I was totally caught off guard and muttered something about how I wasn't aware that I was an alcoholic. He said that it didn't matter, that everything I needed to know about being a pastor I would learn if I went, and that when it came to my turn to share in the meeting I should simply say, "Hi, I'm Rob, and I pass."

So I went, and it changed my life.

As the people went around the room and told their stories, the gears in my mind turned as fast as they could, trying to figure out and name what it was about the meeting that was so different from any other gathering I'd ever been in.

Slowly it dawned on me what it was: I was in a bullshit-free zone.

In that first meeting I went to, people were talking about the first of the twelve recovery steps, which deals with admitting your powerlessness.

Admitting demands honesty.
Admitting requires a ruthless assessment of your condition.
Admitting is what happens when you've hit the wall,
when you have no energy left to pretend,
when you're done playing games,
when you no longer care what other people think,
when you've come to the end of yourself,
when you're ready to embrace the truth that you need help, and that on your own you're in serious trouble because you've made a mess of things.

As I sat there, it was as if I could see, really *see*, for the first time, just how much time and energy and effort we expend making sure that everybody knows how strong, smart, quick, competent, capable, together, and good we are. (I imagine you could add your own words to that list.)

It's hard to see just how much that posturing consumes us until you're in a room where it's absent—a room where people aren't doing any of that because they are giving their energies to *admitting*.

Our need to control how others see us is like a god we've been bowing down to for so long we don't even realize it. But in an AA meeting, no one has energy left for that sort of thing. You come face-to-face with yourself as you truly are.

And now here's the twist,
the mystery,
the unexpected truth about *admitting* that takes us back to the counterintuitive power of gospel:
When you come to the end of yourself, you are at that exact moment in the kind of place where you can fully experience the God who is for you.

I was at dinner recently with a friend who is very clear about how religious she *isn't*. She was telling about her daughter's recent health scare and how terrifying it had been for her as a mother and how all she could do was pray, even though she doesn't pray.

Why do people who don't pray, pray when they're terrified?

I tell you about my friend sitting there at dinner sharing that story about praying because when we talk about the God who is *for* us, we first have to talk about our deep-down, intuitive awareness that we need help.

I realize that this sort of talk is out of sync with many of the dominant voices that have been working on us for a number of years now, insisting that we are the answer to our problems, that there is no one else out there, and that if we don't fix things ourselves, there are no other options. While this sounds empowering and reasonable and free from all that primitive religious superstition, what we actually run into in the course of our everyday lives are endless struggles that (if we're honest) we need help with if we're going to survive, much less prevail, because on our own we know that we are powerless.

From lying to explosive anger to addiction to the inability to forgive to overwhelming helplessness in the face of tragedy to the constant, gnawing anxiety that won't go away to the haunting sense that you're not good enough no matter how hard you work and what you achieve, when we're talking about God, we're talking about the very real sense we have that we do not, on our own, have everything we need and we are not, on our own, everything we could be.

It's there, in that place—naming it and owning it and facing it and going around the room admitting our powerlessness—that we discover the God who has been *for us* the whole time.

Which takes us to the dusty, messy, bloody, and unexpected stories about Jesus,
who
touches lepers, whom no one else would touch,
and
hears the cry of blind people, who had been told to be quiet,
and
dines with tax collectors, whom everybody hated,
and
talks with thirsty, loose Samaritan women he wasn't supposed to talk with—
over and over again we see him going to the edges, to the margins, to those in trouble, those despised, those no one else would touch, those who were ignored, the weak, the blind, the lame, the lost, the losers.

He moves toward them;
he extends himself to them;
he reaches out to them;
he meets them in their place of pain, helplessness, abandonment, and failure.

He is living, breathing evidence that God wants everybody, *everyone,* to be rescued, renewed, and

reconciled to ourselves, our neighbors, our world, and
God.

There are, of course, consequences to his
teaching
and
touching
and
talking
and
dining
and
healing
and
helping.

In his insistence that God is for everybody, Jesus
challenged the conventional wisdom of his day that God
is only for some.
In his standing in solidarity with the poor, he confronted
the system that created those kinds of conditions.
In his declarations that God can't fit in any one temple,
he provoked those who controlled and profited from that
very temple.

All of which led to his arrest, trial, and execution on a
cross. You cannot bring a fresh, new word about human
flourishing and expect the old, established systems of

oppression and power to stand by passively. Or, as Jesus put it, "You can't put new wine into old wineskins."

Have you experienced this? You tried to do some new work, project, initiative—maybe it was in a school or a hospital or a neighborhood or a faith community—and you kept running into a brick wall of resistance. You saw a need and you did your best to meet it, only to encounter and be beaten down by those with a vested interest in things remaining exactly as they are.

I ask you about your own experiences of resistance to human flourishing because there's a moment when Jesus first tells his followers that he's going to be killed. They don't get it: they push back, they resist his prediction, because they assume that he's come to win, not lose. To prevail, not surrender. To conquer, not hang on a cross.

They say no because they've come to believe that he is in some way *God-among-them,* and what kind of God *fails*?

It's all upside down,
backward,
not how it was supposed to be.

And that, we learn, is the point.

———————

On the cross, suffering the worst a person can suffer, Jesus asked, "My God, my God, why have you forsaken me?"

It's a question,
but it's also a window into a whole new way of understanding God.

What we learn from Jesus, what we see in his pain, abandonment, and agony, is that God is there, too.

God is in the best,
and also in the worst.
God is in the presence,
and also in the absence.
God is in the power,
and also in the powerlessness.

God is there, too.

God is there in the tears, the questions, the despair, the blood, the lament—God is there, sitting with us in the ashes, when we shake our fists at the sky and declare that there is no God.

This is the unexpected subversion of the cross, turning so many of our ideas about God on their heads, insisting that God is so *for* us that God is willing to take on the worst the world can bring and suffer it, absorb it, and feel it, right down to the last breath.

We are free—

free to make choices and exert our will and inflict all
kinds of pain and abuse on ourselves, each other, and the
environment.

Which is what we've done.

In Jesus we see the God who bears the full brunt of our
freedom, entering into the human story, carrying our pain
and sorrow and sin and despair and denials of God,
and then,
as the story goes,
being resurrected three days later.

For the first Christians,
that was the compelling part,
the unexpected twist on Jesus's life,
the ending that's really a beginning.

They saw in Jesus's resurrection a new era in human
consciousness, a new way to see the world being birthed,
a way in which even death does not have the last word.

This is why we are moved by soul music,
with its ache and tremor and naked vulnerability.
This is why we cheer for underdogs, misfits, and black
sheep.

This is why we love to hear stories about people who were rejected and forgotten and abandoned, only to rise up and do something grand and daring and magnificent.

Those songs and stories and underdogs speak to our need to be constantly reminded that it isn't over, the last word hasn't been spoken—a savior dying on a cross isn't the end, it's just the start.

And so when I talk about God, I'm talking about the Jesus who invites us to embrace our weakness and doubt and anger and whatever other pain and helplessness we're carrying around, offering it up in all of its mystery, strangeness, pain, and unresolved tension to God, trusting that in the same way that Jesus's offering of his body and blood brings us new life, this present pain and brokenness can also be turned into something new.

The peace we are offered is not a peace that is free from tragedy,
illness,
bankruptcy,
divorce,
depression, or
heartache.
It is peace rooted in the trust that the life Jesus gives us is deeper, wider, stronger, and more enduring than whatever our current circumstances are, because all we see is *not* all there is and the last word about us and our struggle has *not* yet been spoken.

There is great mystery in these realities,
the one in which we are strong when we are weak,
the one in which we come to the end of ourselves,
only to discover that God has been there the whole time,
the God who is **for** us.

———————

So, having talked about the God who is for us, a few
thoughts to wrap this chapter up.

I'm continually shocked, even though I shouldn't be by
now, by how many people I interact with who see the
Christian faith as something
over and against
and even
in opposition to
human flourishing.

How did the message about the Jesus who comes among
us to heal us and free us and bless us and teach us how
to be more generous and forgiving and less judgmental
and more compassionate ever turn into something other
than a clear and compelling message about God's desire
for us to flourish in God's good world?

It's complete madness how the Jesus story has been so
thoroughly warped and distorted in our world.

Let's start there, then, with the obvious truth that God is
for our flourishing and thriving and well-being, so much

so that Jesus came among us to give us what we need, to forgive and rescue and empower us to experience new life as God always intended it.

Which leads me to a point about that word *experience*.

When Jesus talked about faith, he talked about fruit: results, change, transformation. You tasting, seeing, encountering, and experiencing the full life of God and never being the same again—that's transformation. You hearing *gospel* and having it change the way you see yourself. You gaining a living, breathing awareness of the love of God and then sharing that love with others.

I began this chapter by talking about the Christmas story, because when we talk about God we're talking about **embodied faith**—faith in which the divine takes on flesh and blood, lies in a manger, touches lepers, rubs mud on people's eyes, and offers people bread and wine. Jesus shows us that ultimate truth and mystery are located in bodies and matter and lips and arms and music and grass and water and eyes and relationships.

That's the movement,
the arc,
the story.
That's what Jesus was talking about.

There is knowledge *about* something, and then there is knowledge that comes from your *experiences* of that something. It's one thing to stand there in a lab coat with a clipboard, recording data about lips.

It's another thing to be kissed.

To elevate abstract doctrines and dogmas over living, breathing, embodied experiences of God's love and grace, then, is going the wrong direction. It's taking flesh and turning it back into words. The first Christians talked about the fullness of God residing in Jesus because the movement of that embodiment goes in a particular direction, that direction being from
idea to skin and bones,
from abstraction to concrete being,
from word to flesh.

Imagine that, after you've read a review of an album, someone asks you questions about that album—asks what the songs sounded like and what the lyrics were about. There's a chance you could answer all the questions about that album
without ever actually hearing the songs.

Jesus comes to help us hear the songs.

Which leads us to another truth about the God who is for us.
In one of his first sermons, Jesus taught his disciples to love their enemies and pray for those who persecute them, because God

causes the sun to rise on the evil and the good,
and sends rain on the righteous and the unrighteous.

Jesus said this in an agricultural setting, one in which
people were acutely aware of their need for sun and
rain to grow their crops so they wouldn't starve. And
everybody had their own personal list of who was good
and who was evil, who was right and who was wrong,
who was righteous and who was wicked.

(Kind of like now.)

Jesus does a shocking thing here, insisting that God
shows no favoritism, that God has been blessing and
sustaining and giving to *all* people, even those who are
opposed to God, from the very beginning.

I point this out because at the heart of Jesus's message
is the call to become the kind of person who is for
everybody. Especially people who aren't Christians. This
is why Jesus talked so much about loving our enemies.
To love God is to love those whom God loves, and
God blesses and loves and gives and is generous with
everybody.

Once again, this is terribly obvious and straightforward.
And yet thoroughly radical.
And desperately needed.

And then one more thought about the God who is for us.
We're all, in one way or another, addicts, aren't we?
Some are addicted to the praise of others,
some to working all the time,
some to winning,
others to worrying,
some to perfection,
some to being right, strong, beautiful, thin . . .
perhaps you are enslaved to your own self-sufficiency,
or drugs
or alcohol
or sex
or money
or food.

I assume you're like me and you have hang-ups,
habits,
tendencies,
sins,
and regrets
that plague you.

Whatever it is,
we all need recovery.

I say this because I believe Jesus comes to set us free
and forgive us, to liberate us from shame and guilt and
judgment and all that holds us back. And the way that he
does this liberating, empowering work in our lives is by

announcing who we truly are and then reminding us of this over and over and over again.

It is a radical word about our true selves, a word so fresh and unsettling and surprising that it requires us to trust that it is actually true, that God is indeed **for** us.

CHAPTER 6

AHEAD

So now, after talking about the God who is **with** us and **for** us, I want to explore with you the God who I believe is **ahead** of us, pulling us forward.

Is this how you've heard God described?
Ahead?
Pulling us *forward*?

Is God progressive, with a better, more inspiring vision
for our future than we could ever imagine,
or is God behind,
back there,
in the past,
endlessly trying to get us to return to how it used to be?

In many ways this is one of the central questions of
our time about *everything:* Is the best future a return
to an imagined pristine era when things were ideal,
or is our best future actually in the future?

In the spring of 2008 I was in Seattle, speaking at an
event with the Dalai Lama and Archbishop Tutu and
a number of other spiritual leaders. The purpose of
the gathering was to talk about how we can teach
compassion to younger generations so that the world will
be more and more a peaceful, less violent place.

It was incredibly inspiring to be there. I clearly remember
sitting there, taking it all in, looking around the room at
all of the extraordinary people from all over the world
from every religion—all of us there out of a shared desire
for a better tomorrow. And then somebody leaned over
and told me there were protesters out in front of the
building.

Protesters?

Who could possibly think *this* was a bad idea?

What sort of people got up that morning and thought
that the best possible use of their energies and talents
and time was to make signs and then go downtown to
demonstrate in opposition to a peacemaking event?

Who's *against* peace?

That's like being against puppies, or flowers, or Taylor Swift.

I asked who was protesting and was told it was a group of Christians.
(Sigh.)

I tell you about that event because God was there, at that event, as God has always been, present with all of humanity, leading and calling and inviting and drawing and pulling all of humanity into greater and greater love and joy and justice and equality and peace. It is possible, then, to be very religious and very committed, as I'm sure those protesters were, and yet be working against the new thing that God is doing.

On the sidewalk, in front of the building,
missing out on what God was up to inside.

Sometimes religions are in harmony with this pulling and drawing and calling and inviting, helping people move forward toward their best selves and a better future for all of us, and sometimes religions work against this pulling and drawing and calling and inviting, resisting the very real work of God's *ruach* in the world.

So where did I get this idea that God is ahead of us?
I got it from the Bible.
Which I've learned, over the years, is surprising for most people to hear. For many in the modern world, the Bible

is one of the central reasons for the backwardness of religion.

God is ahead?
And I found that in the Bible?

Yes, and to talk about that, I'll first take you to several of those violent Old Testament passages, the kind that are generally used as evidence for God being behind. So stay with me, because I want to show you something else at work in those stories, something surprising and compelling that I hope changes the way you understand God.

———————

We'll start with a phrase that I'm certain you've read or heard quoted somewhere along the way. It's found in the second book of the Bible, called Exodus, and it reads,

> But if there is serious injury, you are to take life for life, eye for eye, tooth for tooth . . .

You've heard this phrase before, right—*an eye for an eye, a tooth for a tooth*? We usually hear it quoted when someone's talking about revenge.

You get hit; you hit back.
They bomb us; we bomb them back.
They spread an ugly rumor about us; we ask, "Have you heard what they did last summer?"

It's become a euphemism of sorts, a way of justifying the right to get even and settle the score.

There is, however, another way to read this verse.

The chapter this verse is found in deals with issues surrounding personal injury and property damage. It includes instructions about what to do when someone is kidnapped, the importance of making a distinction between whether personal injury was intentional or not, what happens if there's a fistfight and one person doesn't kill the other but injures him enough that he's confined to bed, what the proper procedure is when someone digs a hole and someone else's animal falls into it. There are even specific instructions on what to do if a person's bull gores someone to death, the key question being: Did the bull have a habit of goring and had the owner been warned?

(And we all know how awkward *that* conversation can be: "Hey Phil? Yeah, Bob here. Am I catching you at a bad time? No? Great. Listen, this will take just a minute, and I don't mean any disrespect and I hope you don't take this the wrong way, but—folks have been talking, and I didn't know if you were aware of it or not, but your bull has been goring some of the neighbor kids lately, and I just thought you should know . . .")

Dead animals and digging holes and pregnant women getting punched and slaves getting their teeth knocked

out—it can all seem quite distant, chaotic, and foreign
. . . unless, of course, you turn on the television any time
of the day, where you'll find a number of shows in which
cameras follow police as they—wait for it—break up fights
and settle property disputes and calm down neighbors
who are quarreling over damaged goods. And then there
are those courtroom shows where people argue their
case for why the other person owes them money for—
wait for it again—property damage and personal injury! It
all sounds quite familiar after all. But I'm getting ahead of
myself—we're still dealing with *back then* . . .

In the midst of all these rules about fistfights and bull
gorings is the line about "an eye for an eye, a tooth for a
tooth," which meant that if someone killed your cow, he
owed you *a* cow, not two cows, not a cow and a horse,
and not a chicken. If you dug a hole and his donkey fell in
it and was injured, you owed him proper compensation
for the injury to that donkey—nothing more, nothing less.

"An eye for an eye, a tooth for a tooth" was another way
of saying that the punishment must fit the crime. It was
a law given to *lessen* violence, and it demonstrates a
profound insight into human nature and the character of
revenge.

Revenge always escalates.

When someone wrongs us, we rarely (if ever) want to
do the same thing back. Why? Because we want to do

something *more* harmful. Likewise, when someone insults us, our instinct is to search for words that will be *more* insulting.

Revenge always escalates.

In the ancient world, this truth about human nature had serious consequences. Someone kills your cow—what's to stop you from killing two or three or four of his cows?

Someone injures your wife—what's to stop you from paying him back with something far more lethal?

"An eye for an eye" was a succinct way of creating a legal barrier to prevent the escalation of violence and injury.

When *we* read this passage in our present context, the wisdom of it is often lost on us because it's in among all that talk of slaves and bulls and people getting teeth knocked out and digging holes in the ground. At first glance it can easily appear to be another example of primitive, regressive culture. But at the time this regulation was given, it was a significant advance in the creation of a less volatile, more civil society.

(I assume some of you are thinking at this point: "Hey wait, we in the modern world aren't that much farther ahead; we're just violent and barbaric in *other* ways." Excellent point. We'll get to that in a moment. And others of you may be thinking, "Actually, 'eye for eye' is reflected in the Latin concept of *lex talionis,* which is the basis of our modern legal system. It's not the least bit dated." Again, good point. You're tracking with me. Well done.)

What sounds like a primitive, barbaric, violent phrase was actually, for its time and place, a step forward.

What we see is God meeting real people in a real place at a real time in history and drawing them forward, calling them to greater and greater *shalom,* the Hebrew word for peace and wholeness and well-being.

Did they still have a long way to go?
Of course.
But in Exodus we see a step forward.

Now let's fast-forward hundreds of years to the time of Jesus, because by his day something destructive had happened to the way this command was understood and interpreted. People would have some violence or injustice done to them, and they would justify their desire for revenge by quoting, you guessed it, "an eye for an eye, a tooth for a tooth." In other words: "I'm just doing to them what they did to me!" (Sound familiar?)

The same verse that was intended to create a fair and just legal system, *lessening* violence and revenge, was by Jesus's day being used to *justify* violence and revenge.

Which leads us to a crucial insight: these were very religious people, deeply committed to the scriptures, who were quoting the scriptures in such a way that those people were actually working against God's purposes in the world.

Imagine that—religious people quoting the Bible to defend actions that were the exact opposite of the intent and purpose of those very same scriptures!

It's possible, then, to be quoting the Bible out of the conviction that you're defending God's way when in fact you're in that exact moment working against how God wants to continue drawing and pulling and calling humanity forward.

And then, to put a finer point on it, it's possible to take something that was a step forward at one point and still be clinging to it later on in the story, to the point where it becomes a step *backward*.

With that said, let's move from the "eye for eye" passage to another passage, this one from the book of Deuteronomy. I'll let you read it through before we go any further:

> When you go to war against your enemies and the Zad D your God delivers them into your hands and you take captives, if you notice among the captives a beautiful woman and are attracted to her, you may take her as your wife. Bring her into your home and have her shave her head, trim her nails, and put aside the clothes she was wearing when captured.

> After she has lived in your house and mourned her father and mother for a full month, then you may go to her and be her husband and she shall be your wife. If you are not pleased with her, let her go wherever she wishes. You must not sell her or treat her as a slave, since you have dishonored her.

Where do we even start? Brutal, isn't it?

What a primitive, barbaric, sexist, demeaning, and degrading passage. How could anyone with an ounce of respect for women find this passage anything but offensive, repulsive, and a giant step backward?

Good point.

Let's break it down a bit.

This is a passage about the spoils of war, a common occurrence in the ancient Near East, where people were constantly going into battle, which meant people were constantly winning, which meant people were also losing, which meant being killed. It was customary that whoever won a battle took whatever had belonged to their (now-dead) adversaries for themselves. Animals, jewelry, tents, food, slaves, and of course wives. According to the conventional wisdom of the day, you were free to do whatever you wanted with the spoils of war because those spoils were all seen as your property. And property was seen as *less* than human, to be used or sold or discarded or abused as you saw fit.

That was how things were done.

It's into *that* world that this passage comes, which lists rules for the spoils of war.

First, taking the woman you found attractive into your home meant you were providing for her. She would have a roof, protection, food, clothes, whatever else she needed.

Second, having her shave her head and trim her nails and change her clothes was to allow her to take on the marks of mourning. She had suffered a horrific loss, and so she was to be given time to properly grieve. Grief is a human emotion, and possessions don't have emotions; spoils of war don't have feelings. To give her time to grieve was to treat her as a *person,* not as a *possession*.

Third, to make her your wife meant she was now a fully functioning member of the household, with responsibilities and rights and position.

And then fourth, when a man in that day was not pleased with a woman, he was free to send her away, into a culture in which she had no rights, no standing, and no form of protection against exploitation. As a result, women who had been sent away often had no option but prostitution. This passage forbids sending a rejected woman away without rights and honor and dignity—a significant deviation from the cultural norms regarding spoils of war, because at the center of it was the simple affirmation that women are people, not possessions.

An obvious truth to us, but a revolutionary one at the time—one that went against conventional wisdom regarding the spoils of war, one that significantly improved the treatment of women.

What is a shocking and offensive cultural practice to us was a groundbreaking advancement at that time.

We look back on this passage and it's clearly a number of steps *backward* for us, but for the original audience, at that time, it was a step *forward*.

Did *that* culture still have a long way to go in their treatment of women?
Of course.
Does *our* culture still have a long way to go in our treatment of women?
Of course.

There is a chain of restaurants called Hooters.
Do I need to say anymore?

————————

What we see in these passages is God meeting people, tribes, and cultures right where they are and drawing and inviting and calling them forward, into greater and greater *shalom* and respect and rights and peace and dignity and equality. It's as if human history were progressing along a trajectory, an arc, a continuum; and sacred history is the capturing and recording of those moments when people became aware that they were being called and drawn and pulled forward by the divine force and power and energy that gives life to everything.

To make it really clear and simple, let's call this movement across history we see in passages like the ones we just looked at from Exodus and Deuteronomy *clicks*. What we see is God meeting people at the click they're at, and then drawing them forward.

When they're at F, God calls them to G.
When we're at L, God calls us to M.

And if we're way back there at A, God meets us way back there at A and does what God always does: invites us *forward* to B.

This is true for individuals, families, tribes, nations, cultures, organizations, institutions, and churches. All of it taking place on a continuum, a trajectory, a God-fueled movement within and through human history.

This bit about the clicks leads us to an obvious truth about the Bible, but one we should point out anyway: the Bible is a library of radically progressive books, books that were *ahead* of their time, books that tell stories about human interactions with the divine being who never, ever gives up on us and never stops calling us and pulling us and inviting us into new and better futures.

Several observations, then, about this divine pull.

First, the dominant sins, structures, systems, and stagnations of each of us and the cultures we live in often *resist* the radically progressive movement of God in the world and therefore hold us back from the growth and flourishing God intends for us.

Here's an example of this resistance, from the book of Genesis, the first book of the Bible. God promises a man named Abraham that he is going to be blessed and that out of him is going to come a great tribe and out of that tribe *the whole world is going to be blessed.*

There's a progression in this promise, a progression that is loaded with implications for our world. Abraham, who doesn't have any children, learns that he is going to be the father of a tribe, a nation. This would have made sense to Abraham, because that's how people in his day understood the world: everybody was part of a tribe and every tribe had a father—an originator, a patriarch. Some tribes wandered and some tribes were more settled and some had lots of possessions and were quite wealthy and some had land and some had large armies and some didn't and some went to war often and others avoided conflict at all costs and some formed alliances with other tribes in order to defend themselves against other alliances of other tribes. *Your* identity as an individual in a tribal culture like Abraham's was found in the *tribe* that you belonged to. (Kind of like college football.)

It's in this tribal-centered culture that God calls Abraham to be the father of a tribe that will be different from all the other tribes.

Abraham's tribe will have a higher purpose than simply their own wealth, preservation, and well-being. Abraham's tribe will exist to bless and benefit all the *other* tribes. God calls Abraham to a new state of being that—and here's the really important part—*includes* tribal identity and preservation but then *transcends* it to a higher calling—a calling beyond just maintaining and protecting his own tribe, a calling to help and bless and elevate all the other tribes.

Abraham's calling isn't just about him,
and it isn't just about his tribe;
it's also about the well-being of **all other tribes.**

The rest of the Bible tells the story of Abraham's tribe— the Jews—and their struggles to live up to their destiny and calling. Even their name, Israel, means "the one who struggles with God." Over time prophets rise up and call Israel back to their destiny, one of those prophets, Isaiah, telling them that they're a "light to the Gentiles." (*The Gentiles* is a phrase that essentially means *everybody else*.) Jesus arrives and what does he teach Abraham's descendants? Don't hide your light; let it shine!

Jesus continually reminds Abraham's tribe of their identity and mission and calling, essentially asking them time and time again, "How did you so badly lose the plot? This was supposed to be your story!"

And many of them don't get it,
because
tribes naturally have a tendency to become all about themselves.

Sound familiar?

Have you ever been part of an organization and the experience soured because you realized there wasn't any larger mission or purpose or motivation beyond its own preservation?

Have you ever heard of a nation becoming so addicted to a particular natural resource that it could not produce enough to meet its insatiable need? But instead of cutting back and going with less, it spent even more resources and used a wide array of questionable and sometimes even violent means to obtain this resource from other countries, at the risk of bankrupting itself and causing the loss of untold life?

These truths about the call of Abraham and Jesus's teaching to his tribe lead us to another truth about the divine pull, one that speaks directly to religious communities. It is possible for religious people who see themselves as God's people to resist the forward-calling of God to such a degree that the larger culture around them is actually *ahead* of them in a particular area, such as the protection of human dignity or the integration of the mind and body or the treatment of women or inclusion of the forgotten and marginalized or compassion or intellectual honesty or care for the environment. Churches and religious communities and organizations can claim to speak for God while at the same time actually being *behind* the movement of God that is continuing forward in the culture around them . . .

without their participation.

Which takes us back to the divine pull, to a truth about the promise to Abraham that leads to a truth about our day: self-centered, our-tribe-above-all-others consciousness is at the root of untold war, conflict, racism, ethnic cleansing, environmental destruction, and suffering in the world, and when we talk about God meeting people in the Bible *back then right where they were,* we must, in the next breath, acknowledge that the promise to Abraham is still unrealized.

The click God was calling *them* to *there and then* is a click we still aren't at *here and now.*

The life-giving *ruach* we see at work in the scriptures is still ahead, because in the Bible we find God ahead, confronting and calling people to a new vision of life together that still hasn't been fully realized, that we still haven't seen fully come into existence thousands of years later.

And that truth leads to one about the human heart: as advanced and intelligent and educated as we are, there are some things about the human condition that have not changed in thousands of years. It's very important that we are honest about this glaring reality. We have progressed so incredibly far, invented so many things, found an endless array of new ways to process and share and communicate information, and yet the human heart has remained significantly unchanged, in that it still possesses the tremendous capacity to produce extraordinary ignorance, evil, and destruction.

We need help.

At this very moment there is a great deal of energy being spent by nations around the world to make sure that certain other nations do not get the capability to use nuclear weapons. The nation that is leading this charge is the United States, which has enough nuclear weapons to blow the world up several times and that, contrary to all other nations, has actually used nuclear weapons in the past, killing tens of thousands of innocent civilians. The United States has around 6 percent of the world's population and possesses a little less than half of the world's weapons. If there were a group of one hundred people, and six of them had half the guns—well, we would have a serious problem.

We need help.

To read the Bible, then, as a book about *those* primitive people who had made a mess of things and how God was calling *them* forward and miss the glaring fact that it's also a book about *us* and *our* desperate need to be rescued and helped and brought forward into a better future is an epic, historic case of seeing the splinter in someone else's eye and not the log in our own.

All of which leads me to a story about Jesus's disciples, who come to him agitated because they saw someone driving demons out in Jesus's name. They tried to stop the man, they tell Jesus, "because he is not one of us."

Driving out demons is a good thing, correct?

I think we'd all agree that the fewer demons we have, the better off our day is, right?

So this man is doing something good, something needed, something healing, and yet according to the disciples, "he is not one of us."

And so they try to stop him.

They do this because, for them, the world is divided up a particular way.

Us. And then everybody else.

However they reached this conclusion, we can assume that their culture and families and a number of other factors had worked together to shape them in such a way that they would try to stop someone from doing good.

Jesus, however, is quite relaxed about the whole thing. He tells them not to stop the man, because "whoever is not against you is for you."

I tell you this story because there's something going on in both the disciples' actions and Jesus's response that has been going on for thousands and thousands of years. We divide the world up and label people and create rules and feel righteous about our traditional or progressive stances. We spend a great deal of time arguing for these positions that we've taken and working to get the words right so that we can best articulate why we take the stand that we do.

Only to discover that whatever God is up to, it's bigger and better and wider and stronger and more inspiring and expansive and liberating than we first imagined.

A careful reading of the Bible reveals a book about people having their minds blown and hearts exploded with a vision for humanity so thrilling and joyous it can't be grasped all at once. It has to be broken down into a step, followed by a step, followed by a step, followed by a step. Click, then a click, then a click.

All of which raises the question: So what's God up to at this moment? What does all this talk about the God who is with us and for us and ahead of us look like in everyday life here in the modern world?

That's a great question,
one that will take another chapter.

CHAPTER 7

SO

So what does it look like?
That's the question, right?

I'm like you: I get to this point in a book like this and I want examples, concrete images, stories, pictures—I want to know how these big ideas actually take on flesh and blood in everyday life.

God with us,
for us,
ahead of us—
that all sounds great,
but what does it look like?

It looks like lots of things, and to talk about a few of those things, we'll first talk about temples, and then we'll talk about bread and wine, and then we'll talk about curtains,

kings,
comedy clubs,
shadows,
depths,
dark matter,
splagchnon,
monkeys,
and furniture.

First, let's go back in history, five or nine or twenty-three thousand years ago to a hill with a pile of rocks on it. A group of people are laying out sheaves of grain on that pile of rocks, which (you realize as you get closer) is an altar. They're laying out this grain on this altar because they've just harvested their crop and they want to show their gods how grateful they are for the food that will keep their families alive for months to come. They've learned over time that for this grain to grow, they need the rain to fall in just the right amounts and the sun to shine at just the right times and the crops to be protected from any disease or animals that might eat the seeds. It takes a lot of good fortune for a harvest to be plentiful, and they are viscerally aware of their impotence in the face of all these potentially destructive forces. And so they've developed this ritual of taking a portion of the crop and offering it back to the rain god and sun god and protector god as a way of saying thanks, as an act of worship, hoping to keep the forces on their side so that they'll continue to have abundant harvests that feed their families.

Now let's jump ahead a few hundred years to that same hill, only now there's a temple next to the altar, and people in robes are taking the sheaves from everyday, ordinary people and placing the sheaves on the altar.

Why a temple? Because as the years progressed and the offerings multiplied, the same questions arose time and time again as people questioned if they were doing *enough*. Maybe they needed to be more hospitable to the gods, more welcoming; maybe if the gods took up residence in their midst, things would go better for them. And so they built a temple, a house for the gods.

But with this growing religious system and its rules and rites came the increasing awareness of how many ways things could go wrong.

A wrong word,
an incorrect gesture,
an offensive act,
a flawed sacrifice—
who knows what would set the gods off?
How do you know that the drought you're experiencing isn't because somebody improperly offered his sacrifice, inadvertently provoking the wrath of the rain god?

And so gradually from among their midst a special class of people emerged, called priests, to oversee all of this ritual and offering. People set apart, devoted to the life of the temple, charged with the responsibility of making sure that everything was done in the way that was most likely to bring the favor of the gods.

Now imagine that you are a young woman and you've just discovered that you're pregnant. You want your child to be healthy and you want the birth to go smoothly, so you decide to go up to the temple to give an offering of some grain and wine to the god or goddess who watches over pregnant women. You want to do everything you possibly can to gain the favor of the childbirth deities.

So you leave your house
and you go up to the temple.
You leave your common, ordinary, everyday space
and you go up to the holy, sacred, divine space,
where you meet with the priests—holy, sacred,
uncommon people set apart from the masses to do the
holy, sacred work of running the temple and organizing
the sacrifices and keeping the gods pleased.

You do this because your life is divided into two kinds of space and time.
There is the sacred,
and there is the common.
There is your house,
and there is the temple.

There is the holy,
and there is the ordinary.
There is the divine,
and there is the everyday.

You would never take your dog into the temple area,
in the same way that you would never expect a priest to
show up at your house to help unclog your drain.

Let's pause here to note two significant things briefly:
One, this emergence of altars and temples and religious
rites in human history wasn't a bad thing; it was an *early*
thing. Early in our evolution we humans became acutely
aware that our existence was at the mercy of forces
beyond our control, like rain and sun and disease and
natural disasters. This was actually a rather sophisticated
development, a click forward, because it was rooted in
the acknowledgment that there are dimensions to reality
that are *unseen*.

To point out the second thing, I take you back there
to the birth of religion, because that early division
between the sacred and the common is alive and well
today. There's a church near where I used to live that
did a survey of its congregation, asking how important
people's *spiritual lives* were to them.

Spiritual lives? As opposed to their *other* lives?

Why do many churches celebrate someone being "called" into ministry but so few celebrate when people are called into law or medicine or business or art or making burritos or being a mother?

I can't tell you how many times as a pastor I have interacted with people who were talking about their job and then said something along the lines of, "You know, it's a normal job, not like being a pastor or doing something *spiritual* like that."

I make these two observations because what we see in the Jesus story is the leaving behind of this division so that human history can move forward. In one of the accounts of Jesus's death we read that the curtain in the temple of God—the one that kept people out of the holiest place of God's presence—

ripped.

One New Testament writer said that this ripping was a picture of how, because of Jesus, we can have new, direct access to God.

A beautiful idea.

But the curtain ripping also means that God comes out, that God is no longer confined to the temple as God was previously.

God, of course, was never confined by a building. The point of the story is that *our understanding* of God *was*.

The Jesus story, then, is a radical new stage, or maybe we could say click, in our understanding of God.

A temple is meaningful and useful and helpful because it gives humans a way of conceiving of the idea of the *holy* and *sacred*. To see something as sacred, you have to set whatever it is apart and name it and label it and distinguish it as sacred. This is because you cannot comprehend *everything* being holy and sacred until you can grasp the idea that *something* is holy and sacred. You have to start somewhere. But if you don't keep going, keep moving, keep evolving, there is the danger that in dividing reality up it will stay divided, leading people to see everything else—everything besides that sacred thing—as common, average, ordinary, and mundane.

You have to construct a temple to teach the idea of holy and sacred, but in doing that you risk that people will incorrectly divide the world up into two realms and distinctions that don't actually exist.

This is why the Jesus story is so massive, progressive, and forward-looking in human history. Jesus comes among us as God in a body, the divine and the human existing in the same place, in his death bringing an end

to the idea that God is confined to a temple because the
whole world is a temple, the whole earth is
holy,
holy,
holy,
as the prophet Isaiah said.

Or, as one of the first Christians put it, *we* are the temple.

There's a new place where God dwells,
and it's us.

For more on this leap in how we understand the nature
of reality, we'll go to another table, this one on the night
Jesus was betrayed. Surrounded by his followers, eating
a last meal, he gave them bread and wine, telling them
that those ordinary foods were his body and blood,
telling them that whenever they gathered and took the
bread and wine it would be an enduring experience for
them of the new life he was giving them through his life
and death and resurrection. In doing this, he was treating
common bread and wine as holy and sacred because for
him *all bread and wine are holy and sacred*. And all bread
and wine are holy and sacred to him because *all of life is
sacred and holy,* and that includes all interactions, events,
tasks, conversations, work, words, and of course jobs.

The ancient sages say that when Moses comes across
the burning bush, he doesn't take his sandals off because
suddenly the ground has become holy; he takes his

sandals off because he's just now realizing that the ground has been holy *the whole time*.

You are on holy ground wherever you are, and Jesus comes to let us know that the whole world is a temple because we're temples, all of life is spiritual, all space sacred, all ground holy. He comes to heighten our senses and sharpen our eyes to that which we've been surrounded by the whole time; we're just now beginning to see it.

Temples, then, and church services and worship gatherings continue to have their place and power in our lives to the degree to which moms and business-people and groundskeepers and lawyers and plumbers and people who stock the shelves of the grocery store and teachers and toll-booth collectors and farmers and graphic designers and taco makers all gather around a table with bread and wine on it to participate in Jesus's ongoing life in the world as they're reminded that all of life matters, all work is holy, all moments sacred, all encounters with others encounters with the divine.

For Jesus,
it's never *just* a job,
a conversation is never *just* an exchange of words,
a meal is never *just* the consumption of food,
because
it's never just
bread

and it's never just
wine.

Jesus doesn't divide the world up into the common and
the sacred; he gives us eyes to see the sacred *in the
common*. He comes to help us see things more, more
how they actually are: that they matter, that they're
connected, and that they're headed somewhere.

———————

It's easy for each new day to become like all our other
days, isn't it?

Wake up and eat, then go to work or school or exercise
or head to the grocery store or return e-mails or walk
the dog or call your insurance agent or take the kids to
soccer practice or write that term paper or watch that
game or mow the lawn or go to the dentist or book that
flight or all of the above—all without forgetting to water
the plants and pick up eggs on the way home before
filling out the expense report and hanging the laundry
before brushing your teeth and going to sleep so that
you can wake up

in order to

do it all over again the next day.

Our days can easily become a blur,
the parts and pieces blending together,

all of it losing its connection and depth and significance;
cut off from any sense that there's *way more going on
here*
until a tree is just a tree,
a conversation merely a succession of words,
a song simply noise in the background,
a job just a way to get a paycheck.

All of it reduced to what it is at its surface, shallow level,
separated from the source.

Which takes us back to that nativity scene, to that baby
Jesus with his tiny balled-up fists, to the insistence of
that choir in that surf shop in their song that the divine
and human can exist in the same place. When we talk
about God, we're talking about the Jesus who comes to
reunite and reconnect us with the sacred depth, holiness,
significance, and meaning of every moment of every day.

Jesus told a story about a king who was making
decisions about his subjects, separating people "as a
shepherd separates the sheep from the goats." The
sheep, we learn, are the ones who brought the king food
when he was hungry and water when he was thirsty and
clothes when he was naked and looked after him when
he was sick and visited him when he was in prison.

The sheep are confused when they learn of their good
standing with the king.

"Uhhhhhhh, king?" they protest. "When were *you* hungry or thirsty or naked or lonely or sick? We've never seen that!" They ask because of course they understand the king to be quite wealthy, not lacking in basic necessities like food, clothing, and friends.

He responds, "Whatever you did for the least of these brothers and sisters of mine, you did for me."

The king here makes the astounding claim that he is somehow present with and standing in solidarity with *all* of them, and that love and care and compassion shown to *others* is love for *him*.

Jesus tells stories like this one often, stories that speak to the divine presence in every single one of our interactions—a unity, power, and love present in all things, hidden right here in plain sight.

This story Jesus told raises the haunting question: What are we missing? Is there an entire world, right here within this one, as close as our breath, but we aren't seeing it because we're moving too fast, we're separated from the source, cut off from the depths, our eyes not as open as they could be?

Jesus comes to help us see things as they truly are, moving forward, with greater and greater connectivity, higher and higher levels of hierarchy leading to holism beyond even us as all matter is permeated by the redeeming energy and power of God.

The first Christians had a way of talking about this massive movement, bigger than any one of us, that's sweeping across human history: they wrote that God is in the process of moving everything forward so that God will be *over all and through all and in all,* and in another passage in the Bible it's written that God does what God does so that God may be *all in all.*

Over
and
through
and
in
and
all in all.

For God to be recognized as all in all,
then, we will become more and more aware of the uniting of all the depths and dimensions of being—
from the physical to the spiritual,
from the seen to the unseen,
from matter to spirit and everything in between—
as we see more and more of the universe as the single, seamless reality it's always been.

As we say yes to this invitation and call and pull, more and more things that were previously thought to be at odds—

like science and faith,
the brain and the heart,
logic and feeling,
joy and suffering,
having explanations and not having explanations—
will become reconciled to each other and take their
proper place
as more and more we flourish and thrive in this life, right
here and right now.

Which reminds me of my friend Tim.

He's a comedian, actor, motivational speaker, and author.
He used to do a radio show on Friday mornings in which
he'd answer callers' questions live on the air as a number
of different characters. One Friday he began talking
on air as an old Irish priest, calling himself Father Tim
and inviting people to ask him anything they'd like to
know. Father Tim was an instant hit, so much so that
Tim decided to make a public appearance at a radio
promotional party. Did I mention that it was a classic rock
station? Wearing a robe and a big round priest hat he'd
found, he showed up at the party and greeted people
and walked around smiling and telling stories, as if it
were totally natural to be dressed as a priest at a classic
rock station promotional party.

Did I also mention that he's absolutely fearless?

One woman told him that her husband had driven an hour to see him in person, adding that she was sure her husband had "never been this close to God." Other people came up to him and asked him to bless their babies.

Tim, it might not surprise you, decided to take it farther. He took a large piece of cardboard and cut a square hole in it; then he took some strips of cardboard and glued them together to make a confessional window in his cardboard confessional wall. Then he went downtown late on a weekend night to a comedy club in full Father Tim robe and hat and asked the stage manager if he could go on. The crowd, as they often are by this time, were quite rowdy, just as Tim prefers them. He went up on stage, sat down in one of two chairs, put the cardboard confessional wall between him and the other chair, and asked if anybody wanted to make a confession.

Here's the fascinating part: they did—lots of them! Within moments people were lined up to publicly confess their sins in front of complete strangers. In a comedy club. Late on a Friday night.

I tell you this story because often we carry around secrets, sins, doubts, regrets, and crippling fears that we simply don't know what to do with. And so those things are in there, in us somewhere, lurking in the shadows, sapping us of strength and vitality.

As it's written in the Psalms,

> When I kept silent,
> my bones wasted away . . .

In spite of all the ways that we live split, detached, and compartmentalized lives, we know that this is not how it's supposed to be, because our bodies and minds and hearts and consciences want to be united. When we're talking about God, then, we're talking about the power pulling us forward, the awareness we have that when something is eating us up inside it's not right to keep it hidden or repressed or stuffed down in there. It's the *ruach* of God, drawing the truth out of us so that those dark and destructive energies are no longer wasting our bones away.

We have phrases for this movement of God in our lives—
we speak of getting something off our chest,
we talk about how good it was to vent,
we say after we've voiced some truth or doubt that we feel a thousand times lighter,
all of this language blurring the line between our thoughts and emotions and bodies.

Why does ranting about how we really feel create such release *in our chest*?

For many, the word *confession* is tied up in what they perceive to be archaic ideas about God and judgment

and condemnation and how bad we are and how God
just can't wait to crush us.

But confession—
confession is about liberation,
freedom,
naming the darkness and pain that lies within and, in
naming it, robbing it of its power.

Jesus told a story about two men who went up to the
temple to pray. One went on and on about how glad
he was for all of the good things he'd done and how he
wasn't like other people, while the other man stood at a
distance and prayed, "God, have mercy on me, a sinner."
Jesus said that the second man went home justified. Or,
as we might say, it's the second man who went home
free.

Confession is like really, really healthy vomit. It may
smell and get all over the front of your shirt, but you feel
better—you feel cleansed—when you're done. Over the
years I've had people confess all sorts of things to me,
from trivial and sometimes even funny to strange and
dark and violent and illegal. I always first ask them, "Have
you told anybody else about this?" and a shockingly high
number of people say no, no one knows about this.

This is not only sad, but destructive. We *need* each other.
We need friends and community, people we can vomit
all over, getting it out, confessing it, and saying yes to

the pull of God forward to live whole, integrated lives, where nothing is split or stuffed or repressed or stifled or hidden.

This is why the Psalms, the collection of prayers in the middle of the Bible, are so full of people asking God to do horrible, vengeful, violent things to their enemies.

You've felt that way before, right? Like you wanted someone who hurt you to suffer in a prolonged, excruciating way? The Psalms show us what a healthy, vibrant spirituality looks like—you pray those impulses, you speak them, you drag them up and let them pass through your lips, however mean and nasty and cruel they are.

And what you discover when you do this is that they become *less* than what they used to be.

Less pressing,
less urgent,
less powerful.
Make a list of every last awful thing you want done to the one you hate, and by the end of your list making you will have far less energy for list making.

Simply by being honest about what's really going on inside of you, you live less and less divided. It's written in the Proverbs that "a heart at peace gives life to the body." Of course. The mind and the heart and the bones and the body are all an interconnected, interrelated whole. When you've wronged someone or violated your true self and it remains a deep, dark secret, it negatively affects *all* of you.

This is what Jesus does: he comes to integrate, to make whole, to take all the bits and pieces and dis-integrated parts and bring them together, reconciling us to ourselves and to the God who never stops inviting us forward—the God who, reintegrating and reintegrated, finally truly is all in all.

We all have a shadow side, the part of us in which our fears and insecurities and greed and terror and worst suspicions about ourselves reside. It's a churning, restless, dark place, often containing truths that can cripple us with just a fleeting thought.

When I talk about the God who is with us, for us, and ahead of us, I'm talking about our facing that which most terrifies us about ourselves, embracing it and fearing it no longer, refusing to allow it to exist separate from the rest of our being, resting assured that we are loved and we belong and we are going to be just fine.

People deal with their shadow side in a number of ways, the most common way being to find outside enemies and point to them, demonizing them and blaming them for long lists of perceived evils. This strategy often does a very effective job of helping us avoid that which lurks within us. Politicians and radio talk-show hosts and pastors can become very skilled in this, constantly pointing out the darkness and evil and twisted ways of others to avoid dealing with the doubts and insecurities and questions they bear in their own bones.

Institutions can easily become shadow management systems, finely tuned to compellingly convince people of how evil, wrong, dangerous, and threatening *somebody else*—some *other* person or group—is.

People often respond favorably to this shadow management because it's much, much easier than actually entering into the darkness. And so the numbers grow, the budget increases, and the system becomes more convinced of its own importance and power, all the while obscuring the unspoken realities that lurk in the center of it: fear, terror, and insecurity. It's easy to crank up the rhetoric, identifying a new enemy each week, calling each one out, appearing to your followers to be strong and authoritative and willing to take a stand, but all of it in the end a weak, shallow, desperate, pathetic, and broken exercise in shadow management.

But as we're more and more open to the ongoing work of God in the world, we become more and more present to our depths.

Remember, 96 percent of the universe is dark matter—
a vibrant, pulsating source of energy for the universe.
We don't transform our shadow side by denial but by
entering into it, embracing it, facing it, and naming it
because we believe God is with us and for us.

When we do this—name our fears and sins and failures
and own up to them, describing them as clearly as we
are able—we pass through them into the new life on the
other side. We have faced the worst about ourselves and
we have survived, making us strong in the only sense that
actually matters. This is why resurrection is so central to
the Jesus story: he faces the worst that can happen to a
person, and comes out the other side alive in a new way.
It is not a false strength we gain, a posing and posturing
and pretending, but a quiet, humble, grounded strength
that has done the hard work of facing our most troubling
inner torments and then watching them be transformed
into sources of vitality and life.

To be healthy and whole, then, will always lead us to
become more and more fully present to our own depths,
which include our shadow side as well as our deepest
desires.

Jesus asked a man, "What do you want?"

A rather simple, straightforward question, and yet how
many can answer it? What is it *you* want? What is it that
you would pay a high price for and endure hardship for

and overcome any obstacle put in your way to have? What is it that would get you up every morning thrilled for another day?

There's a reason why so many personal transformations begin with the question, "Is this all there is?"

God gives us desires,
heart,
passion,
and love—
gives us desires for justice, compassion, organization, order, beauty, knowledge, wisdom—
and when we become separated from these desires, we lose something vital to who we are. For many of us, we learned quickly how to adapt, what authority figures wanted from us, and how to play the game. This can be good, and profitable, and can earn us all sorts of attention and accolades, but this can also violate who we are. We can become enslaved to the expectations of others, losing our true self in the process.

The Greeks had a way of talking about the deep place within us where our desires reside: they called it our *splagchnon*. *Splagchnon* translates literally as *bowels* or *intestines* or *guts* or *innards*. It came to refer to the part of you from which you truly live, the seat of your being that drives you to move and act and touch and feel.

And so when we talk about God, we're talking about the divine *ruach* who is constantly at work in us, connecting us to our *splagchnon,* calling out of us all kinds of resolve and fiber and spine we may not even have known we possessed, giving us what we need to face and know and name and embrace all that is true about us, from our fears and addictions and doubts and guilt to our dreams and desires and hopes and longings.

God, it turns out, is found over, through, and in all of it. Which includes, of course, our bodies.

A friend of mine recently told me about a woman in a small town in the Midwest who started teaching a weeknight yoga class. It was the first yoga class ever taught in her town, yet a surprisingly large number of women began attending. The teacher told my friend that a fascinating thing began happening in the classes: several of the women (different ones each time) would begin weeping partway through the class, and they wouldn't stop.

Now, I assume you're like me when I first heard about that class, and you're thinking, "What's the problem? It's just yoga." But the teacher quickly developed a compelling theory about why the women were crying. Yoga is a Sanskrit word that means to *join, unite,* or *integrate.* As the teacher got to know the participants and listened to their perspectives on the class, she learned that for many of these women, it was the first time they had ever been told that their body is good and that it is proper and healthy for them to honor and respect and care for it as the sacred gift that it is. They'd never had someone guide them in the intentional integration of their body with their rest of their being.

Have you ever known that someone was lying but you couldn't give a very articulate explanation of *how* you knew, other than "I just know"? In an interview with *Harper's Bazaar,* Gwyneth Paltrow talked about a boyfriend she'd had who frequently cheated on her, which she said she "knew on a cellular level," though she "bought his story."

She knew *on a cellular level.*

We tell ourselves that we are rational, logical people, but we *know* a number of things—things we're sure of, positive of, certain of—because of gut feelings, heartfelt inclinations, cells and molecules telling us what's real and what's true.

It's been estimated that our unconscious influences 70 percent of our behavior. We're picking up signals from people and places all day long. We often know when we're being followed, when someone can or can't be trusted, and even when we're being watched. It's astounding how many women know when they aren't safe, even if they can't tell you how they know this. Much of this comes from what's called *subcortical energy,* coming from a place in our bodies other than our rational consciousness.

We are highly perceptive beings, with layer upon layer of sensory complexity, all finely tuned and precisely calibrated to pick up the millions of messages our personal environment is sending us every single second.

This is why art speaks to us so deeply. If you're in a gallery and you're standing in front of a painting and you aren't moving because what you're seeing is so powerful, chances are if I ask you why you're drawn to that painting, you won't be able to explain it to me, other than in vague terms. As the legendary British theologian Keith Richards put it, "There's something primordial in the way we react to pulses without even knowing it."

What happened in the Western world several hundred years ago is that the rational dimensions of our being gained a prominence over other ways of knowing— specifically, over intuition. This had a powerful effect on the way we process external stimuli, leading many of us to discount the very real and reliable information our bodies are constantly absorbing from the world around us.

To be open to the integrating power of Jesus in our lives, then, will mean that we are more and more connected with *all* of the ways we know things, from our linear, logical, intellectual powers all the way down to the hairs on the back of our necks and the tightness in our guts. And this isn't just about listening and trusting our bodies, but also about the far more important responsibility we have to honor them as the gifts they are.

It will not stop there, however, because **the more we are attuned to our own depths and shadows and desires, the more God is all in all in our lives, and the more we realize the depths of interaction between us and others in every gesture, conversation, and interaction.**

In the early 1990s several Italian neurobiologists were studying monkeys and how their brains work. When a monkey ate a peanut, a certain motor neuron in the monkey's brain would light up. But then the scientists learned something else, something unexpected: when the monkey watched one of the researchers eat a peanut, those same motor neurons lit up again.

Just from watching.

Related research on the *human* brain led to the discovery that when person A watches person B eat a peanut, 20 percent of person A's motor neurons light up as if he's eating the peanut himself.

Your **actions cause** ***my*** **brain to act in very specific ways.**

Ever find yourself yawning because your friend just yawned? Ever reach for your glass in a restaurant to take a drink and realize that you're doing it because your friend across the table just took a drink?

Same thing.

We deeply impact each other, and we are way more connected and aware of what each other is doing than any of us realize. We're patterns and relationships of energy, moving through space and time, made of millions of cells that are dying and being replaced every second, along with the trillions of swirling, frenetic atoms that comprise us in this second but in the next will go on to be others.

When we say that we had a draining conversation with someone, who knows what kind of exchange was going on at a subatomic level? That person may actually have been draining us. It may not be just a figure of speech.

When we talk about how that person took a piece of us, did she really?

When we say that somebody sucked the life out of us, how do we know that he didn't do exactly that?

What the modern world did in its fascination with parts and pieces is teach us that we are individual, isolated human units, talking and conversing and interacting but not much more than that. What we intuitively know, however, and what we're learning more and more from current science, is that there's way more going on between us than we first thought.

So when Jesus calls us to love our neighbor, this is more than just a command or an ethical statement or a rule of life; it's a truth about the very nature of reality. We are deeply connected with everybody around us, and our intentions and words and thoughts and inclinations toward them matter more than we can begin to comprehend.

There are different kinds of engagement and drain, and they affect us in much different ways. When a high school student walks out at the end of taking the SATs, her brain is cooked. When you finish a five-mile run or an hour-long weight-lifting session, your muscles ache and you're drenched in sweat. But when your friend's mother dies and you go to the funeral, that's a different kind of fatigue. It drains not so much your brain or your muscles as it drains your *spirit*. Some events exhaust us at a spirit level, in the same way that some people can crush our spirit if we let them. Learning to be present to our depths means paying attention to all interactions and the toll they exact or the life they bring to that most mysterious, elusive aspect of ourselves we call *spirit*.

Remember Einstein's discovery that matter is locked-up energy, and energy is liberated matter? You exert a gravitational pull on every object around you, including people. And they're doing the same, at the exact same time.

When we encounter someone inspiring, it may be way more than words or actions that she gives us. Likewise, when someone makes something for us and then gives it to us and it means something to us and moves us, we feel like a part of that person is present in the gift. It's not because we're superstitious; it's because a part of him may actually be in the gift.

When we talk about the vibes somebody gives off,
or the not-so-good feeling we're getting from someone,
or we're sure that somebody is jealous,
or harboring bitterness,
or distracted,
our bodies are doing the job that highly sophisticated radar systems do, picking up signals and processing them in real time.

Deep, as we know, calls to deep.

Our body language and facial expressions and changes in posture when we're interacting with each other are so vast and varied that some of them can't be consciously noticed until they're videotaped and played back *in slow motion*.

When you have the sense that someone has more to tell you but you don't know how you know that, there's a good chance that her body sent your body that information faster than your mind could notice it.

The brain alone is stunning in its endless ability to process and morph and transform in response to external stimuli. This is called *neuroplasticity,* and from it we learn that how we focus our attention actually shapes our brain.

Joy is contagious,
and despair brings everybody down,
and when positive energy is present and flowing,
we all benefit.

This is why we find so many writings in the scriptures about the fruit of the spirit and not complaining and rejoicing and again rejoicing and being grateful and saying thanks and remembering where we've been. As we are more and more open to Jesus's integrating work in our lives, we are more and more aware that these clichés about positive energy and good vibes and joy being contagious are true facts about how the world works.

Events and environments act on us, and the more we are experiencing God bringing together all the dimensions of our lives, the more we'll be aware of the powerful effect our surroundings and interactions are having on us.

One quick example involving architecture: You are
a phototropic being, drawn to light, for a number of
biological and physiological reasons. But you also have
legs that get tired if you have to stand for too long. So
when you enter a room, you are drawn to the window,
but you are also drawn to the chairs. You want light, and
you also want to sit down. Which is all fine, unless the
chairs are not arranged in front of the window. When that
happens, the room draws you to two places at the same
time. This creates tension in your being, very real forces
within you that are unresolved.

Now think about those contending forces on a larger
scale. As modern consciousness built a head of steam
over the past few hundred years, very real dynamics
such as these were often pushed to the side, because
people saw the universe as more and more of a machine,
engineered to be productive and efficient. Design and
aesthetics and how things look and feel were often
relegated to lesser status, rendered irrelevant because
they were seen as having very little to do with what can
be empirically measured and demonstrated, like profit
and cost and productivity and efficiency.

But we are integrated beings, and aesthetics matter.
The Bible itself begins with God taking great joy in how
things *look*. Color and layout and feel and landscape and
furniture arrangement and shape and form and line
and curve all matter, because they affect us in powerful
and sublime ways.

Beauty matters, and as we are more and more alive to the divine *ruach* at work in the world, the more and more aware we will be of the importance of all dimensions of our being, because Jesus is at work saving and rescuing and redeeming and reconciling all of us, uniting us, bringing us more and more into the full and joyous life God intends for us.

———————

Back once more to that table with the bread and wine on it. There's a reason why people have been taking the bread and wine and remembering Jesus's life and death and resurrection for the past two thousand years.

We need reminders of who we are and how things actually are.

And **so** we come to the table exactly as we are, some days on top of the world, other days barely getting by. Some days we feel like a number, like a machine, like a mere cog in a machine, severed and separated from the depth of things, this day feeling like all the others. Other days we come feeling tuned in to the song, fully alive, hyperaware of the God who is all in all. The point of the experience isn't to create special space where God is, over and against the rest of life where God isn't. The power is in the striking ability of this experience to open our eyes all over again (and again and again) to the holiness and sacred nature of all of life, from family to

friends to neighbors to money and breath and sex and
work and play and food and wine.

That's God all in all, bringing together all of our bodies
and our minds and our souls and our spirits and all the
parts and pieces that make us *us,* as our eyes are opened
in
the good,
the bad,
the ugly,
the beautiful,
the inspiring,
and the
gut-wrenching
to the presence in all of life of the God who is with us,
for us,
and ahead of us.

EPILOGUE

One last thought.

In the New Testament there's a letter that one of the first Christians, a man named Paul, wrote to his friends in a church in a city called Philippi. In that letter he tells them that the God who *began* a *good work* in them will be sure and certain to *complete* it. Paul does something really, really clever here in this letter that many of his contemporary Jewish writers often did: he uses particular words in a particular order so that he can say multiple things at the same time. Paul uses the words *began* and *good work* and *complete* very deliberately: those are loaded words, because they're used in that same order in the Genesis creation poem that begins the Bible, a poem about a massive bang that brought the world into being, bristling with explosive creative potential and possibility. So when Paul, a man thoroughly versed in the ancient Hebrew scriptures, uses those particular words in that particular order in his letter to his friends, he's connecting their story to the creation of the universe.

His point is that **the same creative bang that formed the universe is unleashed *in us through our trust in what God is doing in the world through Jesus*. His insistence is that this extraordinary energy in all its diverse and expansive forms is *deeply personal* and *readily available* and *on our side*.**

I believe this is true.

I believe you and I are only scratching the surface of what's possible.

We're these strange, exotic cocktails of dust and quarks and blood and soul and all that can't be named, containing infinite depth and dimension and spirit, featherless bipeds arguing and dividing ourselves up about all sorts of things that are, in the end, completely meaningless.

I sometimes wonder if it's as simple as saying *yes,*
over and over and over again,
a thousand times a day.

It's not a complicated prayer, less about the words than about the openness of your heart, your willingness to consider that there may be untold power and strength and spirit right here, right now, as close as your next breath. This isn't about the same old message of making something happen; it's about waking up to that which is already happening, all around you all the time, in and through and over you, trusting that God is with us and for us and ahead of us.

———————

One morning recently I was surfing just after sunrise, and there was only one other surfer out. In between sets he and I started talking. He told me about his work and his family, and then, after about an hour in the water together, he told me how he'd been an alcoholic and a drug addict and an atheist and then he'd gotten clean and sober and found God in the process. As he sat there floating on his board next to me, a hundred or so yards from shore, with not a cloud in the sky and the surface of the water like glass, he looked around and said, "And now I see God everywhere."

Now *that's* what I'm talking about.

ACKNOWLEDGMENTS

I continue to find it pure joy to work with the fine folks at HarperOne. Their integrity, wisdom, passion, and excellence are extraordinarily inspiring to me. When I talk about them, I'm talking about Mark Tauber, Claudia Boutote, Michele Wetherbee, Laina Adler, Kathryn Renz, Suzanne Wickham, Darcy Cohan, Lisa Zuniga, Terri Leonard, and of course the one and only Mickey Maudlin, whose editing, endurance, and friendship mean the world to me.

And to think, we're just getting started.

A big shout as well goes to Tim Green at FaceOut Design, Chris Ferebee for twelve years of guidance, expertise, and fantastic salsa, and Rob Strong, Dr. Christopher Hall, and Dave and Sarah Vanderveen, Glenn Rogers, and the Mighty Iris, who provided valuable feedback along the way. And yes, Glenn, I'm including the time you fell asleep on the deck in Mexico late at night while I was reading an early draft of a chapter out loud. I will continue to attribute your actions to the strength of tequila and not the quality of the content.

And then K, for way too many things to mention. Where exactly would I be without you?

RESOURCES, NODS, NOTES, AND A FEW SHOUT-OUTS

The Title

. . . is a nod to the Japanese novelist Haruki Murakami's memoir, *What I Talk About When I Talk About Running*, which is *his* nod to a Raymond Carver short story collection, *What We Talk About When We Talk About Love*.

Hum

The *familiar/unfamiliar* line echoes Dallas Willard, who begins his masterful book *The Divine Conspiracy* talking about Jesus and how "presumed familiarity has led to unfamiliarity, unfamiliarity has led to contempt, and contempt has led to profound ignorance."

The story about Jacob waking up is from Genesis 28.

The Helmut Thielicke quote is from *The Trouble with the Church*.

For a spot-on analysis of the God problem, see Andrew Sullivan's stunning essay at www.thedailybeast./newsweek/2012/04/01andrew-sullivan-christianity-in-crisis.html.

God never existed in the first place. In regard to the question "Does God exist?" Huston Smith makes a helpful distinction between *absence of evidence* and *evidence of absence* in *The Soul of Christianity*.

The quotes from Jane Fonda and her interviewer are from the June 2007 anniversary issue of *Rolling Stone* magazine.

Ground of our being is a phrase from Paul Tillich.

If you are new to Banksy, I suggest first you read his book *Wall and Piece* and then see his film *Exit Through the Gift Shop*. You will never be the same again.

I'm aware that *withness* and *forness* aren't really words. Until now, of course.

Open

When it comes to the "Those things don't happen" discussion, I suggest Yann Martel's book *The Life of Pi*.

I first talked about some of the ideas in this chapter in my 2007 live film *Everything Is Spiritual,* which you can find at robbell.com.

I. Welcome to the Red Shift

The word *universe* comes from two Latin words, *unus,* meaning *one,* and *versus,* meaning *to turn*—that is, "turned into one."

If you're interested in learning more about the universe but you want to read only one book, I suggest Bill Bryson's *A Short History of Nearly Everything*. He manages to make a staggering amount of information endlessly fascinating, which is an extraordinary gift, to say the least, and one that inspired me in the writing of this book, and especially this chapter.

13.7 billion years. It never ceases to entertain me how this number is often stated with such conviction and precision. Not 13.6 or 13.8, but 13.7. What do those equations look like? How big is that chalkboard? (or whiteboard or computer program or whatever . . .)

Jump off the roof of your house. Often when I'm writing I'll need an example of something and I'll type the first thing that comes to mind and then later go back and read what I wrote and think to myself, "What? Jump off the roof of your house? Who uses examples like that?" Or maybe the better question is "Who jumps off the roof of his house?" The answer is me. I have, on a number of occasions.

Fit in a teaspoon. For more, see io9.com. "What would a teaspoonful of neutron star do to you?"

Black holes, dark matter, and dark energy. See earthsky.org for a large-scale map of dark matter (January 9, 2012, entry; type "large-scale map" in search box).

"Dancing on the Ceiling"? I have no idea why I picked that song. Discussion question for you and your friends: What is the single most overplayed song from the eighties? "Living on a Prayer"? "Girls Just Want to Have Fun"? Do I hear a "Walking in Memphis"?

No things, no time. For more on the relationship between space and time and how it affects the way we understand work and rest, I highly recommend Abraham Joshua Heschel's book *Sabbath.*

Its consistency a persistent illusion is a line from Einstein.

Bendy, curvy, relative. For a mind-bending look at all that curviness, see Leonard Shlain's *Art and Physics.*

Just for kicks, go to answers.com and ask, "How much energy does the sun give off?"

My favorite line from Einstein? "I have a few splendid ideas which now only need incubation."

II. Who Ordered That?

Clearly I'm not a scientist—let alone a quantum or theoretical physicist—so what you find here in this section of the book comes from my having read lots of books by lots of really, really brilliant people. Here are a few I'm most indebted to, both for their insight and their intelligence and, more important, for their ability to make it all accessible to an average chap like me:

> Paul Davies for his book *God and the New Physics* (especially his insights into energy, time, and consciousness)
>
> Lisa Randall for her book *Knocking on Heaven's Door* (which includes a fascinating description of the Large Hadron Collider in chapter 8)
>
> Leon M. Lederman and Christopher T. Hill for their book *Quantum Physics for Poets* (in which they talk about display windows and toasters, among other things)
>
> Fred A. Wolf for his book *Taking the Quantum Leap: The New Physics for Nonscientists*

Several fascinating YouTube clips along these lines:

- Quantum levitation demonstration at the North Museum (Lancaster, PA)
- Russell Brand interviewing a quantum physicist

Grappling with something bigger is from an article on the Higgs Boson in *TIME* magazine, July 23, 2012.

22 quintillion. From Dr. Peter Wittich, Cornell Center for Materials Research (see mr.cornell.edu-Ask a scientist!)

Toaster should glow blue. This is called the Ultraviolet Catastrophe.

III. You Dirty Star, You

Crowned with glory and honor is from Psalm 8.

A great book about being human: *Made for Goodness* by Desmond Tutu and Mpho Tutu.

A great quote about being human: St. John of Kronstadt said, "Never confuse the person, formed in the image of God, with the evil that is in him, because evil is but a chance misfortune, illness, a devilish reverie. The very essence of the person is the image of God, and this remains in him despite every disfigurement."

A great book about the sacred nature of the human body: *Echo of the Soul* by J. Philip Newell.

For more on hierarchy, see Ken Wilber's *A Brief History of Everything,* particularly the first part on nested holons.

For more on what you do with the energies you've been given, see Ronald Rolheiser's fantastic book *The Holy Longing.* The first chapter alone, about Mother Teresa, Princess Diana, and Janis Joplin, will be worth it.

For more on unfolding consciousness across history, see Pierre Teilhard de Chardin's *Activation of Energy.*

IV. The Sea We're Swimming In

Two excellent books on the spiritual implications of quantum theory:

Quantum Leap: How John Polkinghorne Found God in Science and Religion by Dean Nelson and Karl Giberson

Quantum Theology by Diarmuid O'Murchu

One extraordinary book on science and the human spirit:

Einstein's God by Krista Tippett

One brilliant book by a brilliant scientist:

The Language of God by Francis Collins

Principia's original title was Philosophiae Naturalis Principia Mathematica.

It's fun to speculate is from Surfer magazine, April 2012, p. 38.

Both

RQ8F7 double-edged Incisotron. Obviously I totally made that up. But wouldn't you love to have one?

I'm not a businessman is from a remix of "Diamonds Are Forever" by Kanye West.

Because it's there is from "Climbing Mount Everest Is Work for Supermen" interview, New York Times, March 18, 1923.

Where God just was is from Exodus 33.

Saw no form of any kind is from Deuteronomy 4.

Who dwells in unapproachable light is from 1 Timothy. The word unapproachable is the word aprositos in the original Greek—from a meaning not, pros meaning to, and eimi meaning to go—that is, "can't go to."

Spirit is like the wind is spoken by Jesus in John 3.

On plows and hoes, Ken Wilber does a fascinating bit in his A Brief History of Everything.

Can a mother forget . . . ? is from Isaiah 49.

On a side note, in the Genesis poem that begins the Bible, it's written that we are created male and female, "in the image of God." This is important to remember when you encounter churches and religious communities that are run by men and men only, where men do the speaking and leading and decision making. When the female voice is repressed and stifled, the entire community can easily find themselves cut off from the sacred feminine, depriving themselves of the full image of God. Interesting to note that in the Catholic Church, with its all-male leadership, Mother Mary plays such a prominent role. Another example of how the sacred feminine can't be denied; she will express herself *somehow*. She moves, after all, in mysterious ways. (Cue U2 song.)

For more on paradox, see Parker Palmer's classic book *The Promise of Paradox*.

For more on faith and doubt, see Peter Berger and Anton Zijderveld's *In Praise of Doubt*.

Like a tree is a nod to Psalm 1.

Pete's quote comes from *How (Not) to Speak of God* by Peter Rollins.

With

For more on the God who is somewhere else, read John Robinson, who writes insightfully about this in *Honest to God*.

I'm indebted to a number of greater writers for their words about seeing. If you want to read more, I recommend:

> *Everywhere Present* by Stephen Freeman
>
> *God Hides in Plain Sight* by Dean Nelson
>
> *An Altar in the World* by Barbara Brown Taylor

and of course the classic

> *The Practice of the Presence of God* by Brother Lawrence

Massive wall of pink and yellow. The installation is by Peter Wegner and it's called *Guillotine of Sunlight, Guillotine of Shade.* It contains 1.4 million sheets of paper in 40 different colors. For more about Peter Wegner's work, go to petewegner.com.

Ruach occurs over 380 times in the Hebrew Bible.

I can't say enough about Jürgen Moltmann's incredible book *The Spirit of Life,* which has been a huge inspiration to me and helped shape my thinking about *ruach.*

The whole earth is God's. Psalm 24.

God renews the face of the earth. Psalm 104.

On the breadth and power of *ruach* energy, see Psalm 33.

As long as I have life is from Job 27.

The writer in Ecclesiastes uses these words: "And the dust returns to the ground it came from, and the *ruach* returns to God who gave it" (12:7).

On *ruach* garnishing the heavens, see Job 26.

On *ruach* bringing things into existence, see Psalm 104.

Where can I go? is from Psalm 139.

Kavod. The root is K-B-D, and it also means *liver* or *interior* or *soul* or *be important* as well as *heavy*. Hebrew words are quite limber like that. I used it here in a positive sense of something that matters, but much of its use in the scriptures when it's translated *heavy* is negative, as in *oppressive* or *severe* or *a burden*. When it's used positively, it's usually as *glory*, as in 1 Chronicles 16, where David says, "Declare God's glory . . ."

Everything is ultimately connected to everything else. For a stunning example of how everything is connected, see *The Spirit Level: Why Greater Equality Makes Societies Stronger* by Richard Wilkinson and Kate Pickett, in which Wilkinson and Pickett show statistically how the wider the gap between the rich and the poor in a country, the worse off the *rich* are.

The ZadD is one is from the Shema prayer, found in Deuteronomy 6.

Deep calls to deep is from Psalm 42.

Subsurface unity is a line from a commencement speech David Foster Wallace gave at Kenyon College, Ohio, in 2005.

Telos is found forty times in the New Testament.

The Office. It's been fascinating to see the original British series and the arc as it unfolded over two seasons, in contrast with the American version, which in many ways goes the opposite direction.

Seeing and hearing is from Matthew 13.

She has done a beautiful thing to me is from Mark 14.

May the eyes of your heart be enlightened is from Ephesians 1.

For

God loves us is from John 3.

Eight-pound six-ounce newborn infant is from the book of *Talladega Nights*—"Shake 'n Bake, that just happened."

The poor in spirit / blessing is from Matthew 5.

The nobodies is drawn from chapter 4 of Dallas Willard's *The Divine Conspiracy*.

Repent is the word *metanoia* in Greek: *meta* meaning *change* (as in *metamorphosis*) and *noia* meaning to *think* or *perceive*—that is, "to see in a new way, to have a new mind."

Touches lepers is from Matthew 8.

Hears the cry is from Matthew 20.

Dines with tax collectors is from Mark 2.

Talks with . . . Samaritan women is from John 4.

Came for the sick is from Luke 5.

New wine in old wineskins is from Matthew 9.

First tells his followers that he's going to be killed refers to Matthew 16.

My God, my God is from Matthew 27 (which is from Psalm 22).

In regard to the early Christians seeing the resurrection as heralding a new era in human consciousness, note that when the Apostle Paul writes to his friends in Corinth (1 Corinthians 15), he calls Jesus's being raised on the third day something of "first importance."

Jesus talked about . . . fruit draws on Matthew 7 and 13 and John 15.

Fullness of God residing in Christ is from Colossians 2:9.

Causes the sun to rise . . . and sends rain is from Matthew 5.

Ahead

Eye for eye is from Exodus 21.

When you go to war is from Deuteronomy 21. Many thanks to William Webb for his insightful writing on this passage.

There are more than 435 Hooters restaurants in the world.

God calls a man named Abraham. The story of Abraham begins in Genesis 12.

Light to the Gentiles is from Isaiah 49.

Let your light shine is from Matthew 5.

Nuclear weapons. I wrote about this with Don Golden in our book *Jesus Wants to Save Christians*.

Because he is not one of us comes from Luke 9.

A book about people having their minds blown. See Peter's vision in Acts 10.

So

I talked about the birth of religion in my 2008 live film *The Gods Aren't Angry,* which you can find at robbell.com.

Ripped is from Mark 15.

On the concept of new, direct access to God, see Hebrews 10.

Holy, holy, holy is from Isaiah 6.

The idea that God is confined to a temple. I say this while also acknowledging that these ideas were already present in Jewish thought years before Jesus, like in 1 Kings 8 where Solomon says after building the temple that "The heavens, even the highest heaven, cannot contain you. How much less this temple I have built!"

We are the temple is from 1 Corinthians 6.

The reference to the human body as a temple is from 1 Corinthians 6.

Accounts of Jesus on the night he was betrayed are found in Matthew 26, Mark 14, Luke 22, and John 13.

For an extraordinary essay on the Eucharist, see http://www .firstthings.com/onthesquare/2012/03/do-this.

Ephrem the Syrian prayed in the fourth century:

> *The spirit is in your bread,*
> *the fire in your wine,*
> *a manifest wonder,*
> *that our lips have received.*

Stephen Freeman offers profound insights on the Eucharist in his book *Everywhere Present.*

Moses taking off his sandals is from Exodus 3.

Holy the whole time. The word *holy* is related to the word *holistic,* which is connected to the words *whole* and *heal* and *hale* (as in "hale and hearty"). Holiness is the bringing together of things in their entirety, healthy and complete.

Reunite and reconnect us to sacred depth is from Colossians 1, where the Apostle Paul writes that through the shed blood of Jesus, God is reconciling *all things, whether things on earth or things in heaven.*

As a shepherd separates the sheep from the goats is from Matthew 25.

On God as all in all, see 1 Corinthians 15.

On God being through and over all, see Ephesians 4.

Things that were previously thought to be at odds. For more on nondual awareness, read Richard Rohr's *The Naked Now.*

For more on my friend Tim Cusack, go to timcusack.com.

When I kept silent is from Psalm 32.

God, have mercy on me, a sinner is from Luke 18.

For a Psalm about destructive impulses, see Psalm 35.

A heart at peace gives life to the body is from Proverbs 14.

What do you want? is from Mark 10.

Splagchnon is found in the New Testament eleven times.

Knew on a cellular level is from an interview with Gwyneth Paltrow in *Harper's Bazaar,* March 2012.

Something primordial is from Keith Richards's autobiography, *Life,* p. 244.

For more on monkeys and subcortical energy, see Daniel J. Siegel's great book *Mindsight: The New Science of Personal Transformation.*

Talking about *spirit,* Christopher McDougall has a quote in his book *Born to Run* (at the beginning of chapter 30) from the Olympic champion Herb Elliot: "I came to realize that spirit, as much or more than physical conditioning, had to be stored up before a race."

I am deeply indebted to Dr. Tim Royer and the fine folks at Neurocore for all they've taught me about the brain and how it affects every area of our lives.

For more on chairs and windows and sun—on the relationship between architecture and spirit—I highly recommend the following:

The Timeless Way of Building by Christopher Alexander

Between Silence and Light: Spirit in the Architecture of Louis I. Khan by John Lobell

101 Things I Learned in Architecture School by Matthew Frederick.

Fruit of the Spirit is from Galatians 5.

Complaining is from Philippians 2.

Rejoicing is from Philippians 4.

Grateful is from Psalm 18.

Giving thanks is from 1 Thessalonians 5.

Remembering is from Exodus 13, Mark 8.

God taking great joy in how things look is a reference to Genesis 1.

Epilogue

Began / good work / complete is from Philippians 1.

And now I see God everywhere reminds me of the Jesuit saying "Seeing God in all things," which reminds me of a fantastic book about seeing called *Seeing God in All Things: The Jesuit Guide to (Almost) Everything* by James Martin, SJ.

Two Last Notes

Here are some awesome words and phrases and sentences I stumbled upon in my research that deserve to be repeated for no particular reason other than the enjoyment of words and their endless sounds, meanings, and combinations:

relic density

displaced vertex

propensity and power

the history of fishes

the ability of infinity to be boosted in magnitude and yet still remain the same size

a possible planet called Vulcan

the Englert-Brout-Higgs-Guralnik-Hagen-Kibble mechanism

superhuman creative restlessness

breathe deeply and unfurl energies

forms and configurations assumed by the divine spirit's torrent of energy

sounds of all protean creation

planetary regeneration

a radiance which no space can contain

driving vital power

unrestrained speculative exuberance

kinematically

comprehensive reference for life

sensory sociality

permeation of all matter by grace

indescribable elegance

ceaseless becoming

impelling potency

enhanced fluidity

MORE FROM **ROB**

SUNDAY TIMES BESTSELLER

LOVE WINS

AT THE HEART OF LIFE'S BIG QUESTIONS

ROB BELL

With exclusive material from *The Love Wins Companion*

FROM *THE SUNDAY TIMES*
BESTSELLING AUTHOR OF **LOVE WINS**

VELVET ELVIS

REPAINTING THE CHRISTIAN FAITH

ROB BELL

FROM *THE SUNDAY TIMES*
BESTSELLING AUTHOR OF **LOVE WINS**

SEX GOD

**EXPLORING THE ENDLESS
QUESTIONS BETWEEN
SPIRITUALITY AND
SEXUALITY**

ROB BELL

BELL

'He could be one of the most important 21st-century Christian leaders'

TIME